THE GREAT
HISPANIC HERITAGE

Dolores Huerta

THE GREAT HISPANIC HERITAGE

Isabel Allende

Miguel de Cervantes

César Chávez

Salvador Dalí

Gabriel García Márquez

Dolores Huerta

Frida Kahlo

José Martí

Pedro Martinez

Ellen Ochoa

Pablo Picasso

Juan Ponce de León

Diego Rivera

Carlos Santana

Sammy Sosa

Pancho Villa

THE GREAT
HISPANIC HERITAGE

Dolores Huerta

Richard Worth

CHELSEA HOUSE
PUBLISHERS
An imprint of Infobase Publishing

Dolores Huerta

Copyright © 2007 by Infobase Publishing

All rights reserved. No part of this book may be reproduced or utilized in any form
or by any means, electronic or mechanical, including photocopying, recording, or by
any information storage or retrieval systems, without permission in writing from the
publisher. For information contact:

Chelsea House
An imprint of Infobase Publishing
132 West 31st Street
New York NY 10001

Library of Congress Cataloging-in-Publication Data

Worth, Richard.
  Dolores Huerta / Richard Worth.
      p. cm. — (Great Hispanic heritage)
  Includes bibliographical references and index.
  ISBN 0-7910-8838-3 (hardcover)
  1. Huerta, Dolores, 1930—-Juvenile literature. 2. Women labor leaders—United
States—Biography—Juvenile literature. 3. Mexican American women labor union
members—United States—Biography—Juvenile literature. 4. Mexican American
migrant agricultural laborers—Biography—Juvenile literature. 5. Migrant agricultur-
al laborers—Labor unions—United States—History—Juvenile literature. 6. United
Farm Workers—History—Juvenile literature. I. Title.
  HD6509.H84W85 2008
  331.4'7813092—dc22
  [B]

Chelsea House books are available at special discounts when purchased in bulk quan-
tities for businesses, associations, institutions, or sales promotions. Please call our
Special Sales Department in New York at (212) 967-8800 or (800) 322-8755.

You can find Chelsea House on the World Wide Web at http://www.chelseahouse.com

Series design by Terry Mallon/Keith Trego
Cover design by Keith Trego

Printed in the United States of America

Bang EJB 10 9 8 7 6 5 4 3 2 1

This book is printed on acid-free paper.

All links and Web addresses were checked and verified to be correct at the time of
publication. Because of the dynamic nature of the Web, some addresses and links
may have changed since publication and may no longer be valid.

Table of Contents

1   Strike in Delano   6

2   The Early Years   17

3   Community Organizing   27

4   Building the Farm Workers Association   39

5   Fighting the Teamsters Union   48

6   The Success of the UFW   62

7   New UFW Leadership   72

8   Battling for Justice   80

Chronology and Timeline   89

Notes   92

Bibliography   95

Further Reading   96

Index   97

Strike in Delano

In September 1965, grape workers in the large vineyards of Delano, California, went on strike. The workers were immigrants who were paid only $1.00 an hour for picking grapes—far less than the national average in the United States. Harvesting grapes was a back-breaking job that required workers to spend long hours in the hot California sun. They were expected to work quickly, bringing in the grape harvest before the fruit rotted on the vines.

For decades, poorly paid immigrants had worked the harvests. Some of the workers came from the Philippines (Filipinos), but most were farmworkers from Mexico. They harvested grapes as well as melons and strawberries, and vegetables like broccoli, mushrooms, and asparagus. Fruit and vegetable fields stretched across California, Florida, and states in the Southwest. While workers in other industries received more than 10 times as much money as the farmworkers, owners of large farms refused to raise the wages of their field hands. The owners realized that they could get a steady supply of workers from Mexico, where the cost of living was very low. Many of these workers were delighted to earn a dollar an hour. They took the money back home to Mexico to support their families. Jobs were scarce south of the border, and even this small amount of money was welcome.

Three years before the strike, an association of farmworkers had been formed to try to improve working conditions in the fields. Called the National Farm Workers Association (NFWA), it was led by César Chávez and Dolores Huerta. Both were Mexican immigrants, and both of their families had labored in the fields as migrant workers. In 1965, their association was small, with only about 1,200 members. Huerta, who had seven children, had given up her steady income from another job. She received little or no money from the NFWA and lived with her children in the Chávez home. Huerta had taken a giant risk in founding the NFWA. There was no guarantee that it would succeed or that she could adequately support her children.

Neither Huerta nor Chávez was certain whether the time was right for them to begin a farmworkers' strike. If they did not support the Filipino grape workers, however, then the NFWA might lose the support of its own members. Huerta and Chávez called a meeting of the NFWA, which voted overwhelmingly to support the Filipino workers.

The NFWA focused its strike at vineyards owned by the giant Schenley Company, a maker of wines and liquors. As the picketers arrived at the huge 4,500-acre (1,821-hectare) Schenley vineyard, they carried signs that said "*Huelega*" (a Spanish word for "strike").

Some workers who were not NFWA members honored the picket line and did not go into the fields to harvest grapes. But others marched right past the pickets. Chávez, who believed strongly in nonviolence, told the strikers not to use any physical force to stop the strikebreakers. He told NFWA members to use megaphones to urge the grape pickers to stop working, but said they should not do anything more.

Dolores Huerta, pictured here in Delano, California, with César Chávez during the grape pickers strike in 1968, helped Chávez establish the National Farm Workers Association (NFWA) in 1962. Huerta and Chávez were instrumental in making the American public aware of the difficult working conditions endured by farmworkers.

The Schenley Company and other large growers were outraged by what the NFWA was trying to do. The growers tried to undermine the strike by bringing in scabs—nonunion workers who refused to honor the picket line. Chavez led some of his strikers to the homes of the scabs. There, they sang songs and said prayers, trying to convince the scabs to join the strike.

One afternoon, when Huerta was driving home from the picket line, her car had engine trouble. She stopped at a nearby house for help. Instead, she was greeted by an angry grower who chased her away with a gun.

The growers brought in local police to guard their fields. The police tried to keep the strikers away from the field workers and protected the strikebreakers who went in to pick the grapes. Nevertheless, the strike grew. Chávez and Huerta went to local college campuses to gather support for the strike from college students. Some of these students had been involved in the civil rights movement. During the early 1960s, they had marched with Reverend Dr. Martin Luther King, Jr., and other black leaders, demanding equal rights for African Americans. Huerta spoke passionately about the plight of the farmworkers and how they were suffering from injustice just like African Americans. As a result, many students joined the strike.

Other volunteers came from black civil rights organizations, such as the Congress of Racial Equality (CORE). In addition, local clergy joined the picket lines. Publicity for the strikers grew as major newspapers covered the strike and the pickets around the grape fields. Pictures of Dolores Huerta appeared in several publications, including a Communist newspaper. Communist groups in the United States had ties to the Soviet Union (now called Russia), which was run by a Communist dictatorship. The Federal Bureau of Investigation (FBI) believed that Huerta was "the driving force on the picket lines of Delano . . . and daily inspires the pickets and their cause."[1] The FBI began investigating Huerta for possible Communist connections.

The strike continued through the grape harvest season. While the growers successfully brought in their harvests with scab workers, publicity focused on the underpaid Mexican workers who were being exploited by the huge growers. On Friday nights, the strikers would gather together to review the week's events. They would sing and watch comedy skits performed by an acting troop called Teatro Campesino. "I loved the Friday night meetings," one of the strikers recalled. "They were like revivals."[2] These meetings built a sense of unity among the strikers. They felt like more than just a small group of striking immigrant workers. They had become a movement.

THE MOVEMENT GROWS

The strike continued during the cold winter months of 1965–1966. The farmworkers gained support from the powerful United Auto Workers union (UAW). Their president, Walter Reuther, marched with the strikers in California. The union also donated several thousand dollars each month to help support the strikers while they were not working. In March 1966, the Senate Subcommittee on Migratory Labor arrived in Delano to hold hearings on the plight of the farmworkers. The

EL TEATRO CAMPESINO

The Campesino Theater, or *El Teatro Campesino*, was founded by Luis Valdez in 1965, during the strike by the National Farm Workers Association in Delano, California. Valdez, a theater director, approached César Chávez and asked if he could put on skits for the strikers. Chávez agreed, so Valdez and his actors began putting on performances from flatbed trucks near the picket lines. Many of the skits were humorous, featuring characters such as the Mexican-American farmworker, the grower, and the scab. These skits provided entertainment for the strikers after a long day on the picket lines. They also delivered a message about the significance of the strikes to workers, many of whom could not read or write. From its beginnings in Delano, El Teatro Campesino expanded its performances. Over the next few years, its skits focused on the Vietnam War and the importance of the Mexican-American heritage as part of American culture. Valdez also wrote popular plays that were performed in Los Angeles and on Broadway in New York City.

press coverage focused on Senator Robert F. Kennedy, who directed sharp questions at police who had tried to stop the strike by arresting strikers.

Later in March, César Chávez led a 300-mile (483-kilometer) march from Delano to the California state capital at Sacramento. The march was intended to further publicize the working conditions of farmworkers. Chávez also wanted to convince California's governor, Edmund G. Brown, to support legislation that would force the large growers to pay farmworkers a fair wage. The march was similar to the demonstrations that had been led by Reverend Martin Luther King, Jr. across the South to end discrimination against African Americans. Chavez and his followers carried the NFWA's flag—a black eagle in a white circle on a red background. The march occurred during the Christian season of Lent (the 40 days leading up to Easter). The marchers carried a large cross and held prayer services. Meanwhile, cameramen filmed the marchers, and the film footage was broadcast on network news programs throughout the United States.

The publicity eventually became more than the Schenley Company could handle. The company decided that the situation was costing too much money and was hurting its reputation. As a result, Schenley representatives agreed to sit down with the NFWA to negotiate a new contract for the farmworkers. The NFWA negotiating team was led by Dolores Huerta. As a result of tough bargaining by Huerta and her team, the workers received a pay raise of 35 cents an hour. It was the first step on the NFWA's road to success.

THE STRIKES CONTINUE

The Schenley strike was a strong beginning, but Dolores Huerta knew that there were other, tougher growers that the NFWA would still have to face. Among them was the large DiGiorgio Fruit Corporation. In the past, workers had gone on strike at DiGiorgio, only to be fired from their jobs as the company brought in scabs from Mexico. DiGiorgio also called on the power of the local police, who did not hesitate to beat up strikers and drag them off to jail.

In 1966, the NFWA began a strike against DiGiorgio. Huerta went to the Mexican border to stop the company from bringing in scabs. "I was there for a whole month picketing the border, passing leaflets in Juarez, Mexico, and asking people not to work for DiGiorgio," she later said. "Sometimes they were sending two buses every other day to bring in scabs and break the strike. Our work was effective. A lot of the people would get on the bus, and as soon as they got to California, they'd leave the company."[3]

Meanwhile, field workers began walking off the job at a large DiGiorgio vineyard to join the NFWA. It appeared that the company, like Schenley, would be forced to bargain with the workers. DiGiorgio, however, decided to negotiate with another union, the Teamsters, which was opposed to the NFWA. The powerful Teamsters promised to keep the grape workers under control and not demand as much as the NFWA. To combat the Teamsters, Huerta went to Sacramento, where she helped convince Governor Brown to stop the negotiations until the vineyard workers were given an opportunity to decide which union they wanted to represent them. In an election, the vineyard workers overwhelmingly voted to join the NFWA.

A new contract gave the workers more money, as well as some health insurance and paid vacations. No farmworkers had ever achieved benefits like these in the past. DiGiorgio had also been pressured by a new tactic: the grape boycott. NFWA volunteers went to New York and other cities, where they organized demonstrations around large stores that sold DiGiorgio grapes. Many customers refused to buy them.

Other growers saw what was happening at DiGiorgio and also agreed to sign contracts with the NFWA. Once again, the NFWA negotiating team was led by Huerta. As a former schoolteacher, Huerta "had trained herself in the fundamentals of contracts, [and] was in charge of this blitz of negotiations,"[4] according to historians Susan Ferriss and Ricardo Sandoval.

She negotiated contracts with large vineyards like Gallo Winery, Christian Brothers, Almaden, and Paul Masson—all of them well-known manufacturers of wines.

Huerta was exhausted by the nonstop negotiations. After they ended, she collapsed. She said, "The next day I ended up in the hospital. I fainted. I can't remember what had happened a couple of nights before. . . . I had to stay in bed for about three days."[5]

THE GRAPE BOYCOTT

Although the strikes had been successful so far, the NFWA union still had a long way to go before they achieved success. Out of approximately 250,000 farmworkers in California, only about 5,000 were covered by the new contracts. After negotiating with the winemakers, the NFWA went after large growers that provided grapes to American supermarkets, where they were purchased by consumers. The largest grower was the Guimarra Vineyards in California. As Huerta put it, "If we can crack Guimarra, we can crack them all."[6] But Guimarra was tough. The company agreed to increase workers' wages to stop the strike. They also brought in scabs.

To combat Guimarra, the NFWA turned back to the grape boycott. Grapes were harder to boycott than wines, however. Growers could ship and sell their grapes under a variety of labels that were hard to track. To help publicize the boycott, César Chávez began a 25-day fast on February 15, 1968. Some of his followers did not support the fast. As Dolores Huerta explained,

> A lot of people thought Cesar was trying to play God, that this guy really was trying to pull a saintly act. Poor Cesar! They just couldn't accept it for what it was. I know it's hard for people who are not Mexican to understand, but this is part of the Mexican culture—the penance, the whole idea of suffering for something, of self-inflicted punishment. It's a tradition of very long standing. In fact, Cesar has often mentioned in speeches

that we will not win through violence, we will win through fasting and prayer.[7]

Meanwhile, Guimarra tried to stop the NFWA grape boycott by claiming it was illegal and bringing Chávez into court. This simply brought more publicity to Chávez's fast, which was patterned on the highly successful approach used by Mohandas Gandhi to achieve independence in India in the early part of the twentieth century.

On March 11, Chávez broke his fast in a widely publicized meeting with Senator Robert F. Kennedy, who had decided to run for president of the United States. Kennedy championed many of the goals of the NFWA. The meeting between Chávez and Kennedy focused even more attention on the grape boycott.

Meanwhile, the boycott continued in major cities across the United States. Huerta went to New York City, where she persuaded local unions to stop grapes from being unloaded on the New York docks. The unions sympathized with the NFWA because they had battled huge employers and knew how hard it was to beat them. Volunteers from colleges picketed local supermarkets. Housewives were also enlisted in the effort. They walked into supermarkets, selected grapes, and then complained to the manager that the fruit was probably picked by scab workers. This created negative publicity for the store, persuading other customers to leave and not return to shop there. At the same time, colleges and other organizations with cafeterias refused to buy grapes, and sales in New York dropped tremendously.

According to historian J. Craig Jenkins, "By the end of the 1968 season, the boycott was showing its teeth. Retail grape sales were down by twelve percent nationally and by over half in major cities like New York, Boston, and Baltimore. An estimated $3–4 million of grapes rotted on the vines for want of a market outlet."[8] According to a poll taken by Louis Harris and Associates, as many as 17 million people eventually stopped buying grapes. But the growers were not finished. They started a huge advertising effort to encourage consumers to buy grapes.

In June 1968, Senator Kennedy was assassinated. His death occurred shortly after he had won California's presidential primary with the help of the NFWA. Just before the assassination, Huerta had appeared with Kennedy at a hotel in Los Angeles, where Kennedy had announced his victory. In November, Republican candidate Richard Nixon was elected president. Nixon ordered the Department of Defense to buy thousands of boxes of grapes from the California growers to help them defeat the NFWA boycott.

But the NFWA did not stop its efforts. The strikes and the boycotts continued. In a Boycott Day Proclamation, the workers proclaimed:

> We have been farmworkers for hundreds of years and pioneers for seven. . . . But we are still pilgrims on this land, and we are pioneers who blaze a trail out of the wilderness of hunger and deprivation that we have suffered even as our ancestors did. . . . If this road we chart leads to the rights and reforms we demand, if it leads to just wages, humane working conditions . . . if it changes the social order that relegates us to the bottom reaches of society, then in our wake will follow thousands of American farmworkers. Our example will make them free.[9]

The growers were receiving pressure from large supermarket chains to sign an agreement with the workers' union. Meanwhile, the boycott continued throughout the fall, cutting into the growers' profits. By the middle of 1969, the growers claimed to have lost as much as $25 million. By the following summer, the growers had finally had enough. They signaled that they were ready to negotiate with the NFWA.

Once again, the negotiations were handled by Huerta, who brought field workers into the contract talks so they could approve of the agreement. The growers were outraged that

People who worked in California grape fields like the one pictured here often faced terrible working conditions for low pay. Their plight helped win the support of Dolores Huerta and César Chávez and their National Farm Workers Association.

they were expected to deal directly with ordinary field hands. Still, they finally negotiated a new contract, which included higher wages for the workers and employer contributions to a health-care program. As the agreement was signed on July 29, 1970, the workers shouted, "*Viva la huelga! . . . Viva César Chávez!*"[10]

Although the workers shouted for Chávez, the victory at the negotiating table had been achieved by Dolores Huerta. Huerta had played a key role in the founding of the NFWA and in achieving its victory over the huge growers—a major victory for farmworkers who had been oppressed for so many years. Huerta understood their suffering because she had experienced it herself. As a Mexican American, she had been forced to deal with poverty and prejudice in order to achieve the same rights as other American citizens.

2

The Early Years

Dolores Fernandez (later Dolores Huerta) was born in the small town of Dawson, New Mexico, on April 10, 1930. Both of her parents, Alicia and Juan Fernandez, were Hispanic. Alicia's family came from New Mexico, but Juan's parents had emigrated from Mexico.

Spanish settlers first began to arrive in Mexico during the early sixteenth century. They conquered a powerful group of Native Americans known as Aztecs. After establishing a capital in Mexico City, the Spanish began to explore the territory to the north. During the late sixteenth century, settlers came to present-day New Mexico, led by Juan de Oñate, a well-to-do mine owner. He crossed the Rio Grande into New Mexico in 1598. Spanish missionaries also traveled to New Mexico to convert the local Native Americans to Christianity. By the mid-seventeenth century, the Spanish had built about 100 *pueblos*, or towns, in New Mexico and founded a thriving community at Santa Fe. The Spanish settlements were controlled by the government in Mexico City. Other pueblos were built in present-day

17

Santa Fe, New Mexico, which means "Holy Faith" in Spanish, was founded by the Spanish in 1598. The town served as the capital of the New Spain province of Nuevo México until Mexico gained its independence from Spain in 1821.

Texas, Arizona, and lower California. They formed part of the Spanish empire known as New Spain.

New Mexico remained part of the Spanish Empire until the 1820s, when Mexico became independent from Spain. The Mexican government continued to control New Mexico until the 1840s. In 1845, war broke out between the United States and Mexico. Very few Mexican troops defended New Mexico, and it was easily conquered by the U.S. Army. American forces set up their headquarters at Santa Fe.

By 1850, when New Mexico became a territory of the United States, the population was more than 70,000. More Mexicans crossed the border into New Mexico, which continued to grow during the rest of the nineteenth century. A few American settlers also came to the area and married local residents. Some of the settlers owned small farms, but many others worked for large Mexican-American cattle and sheep ranchers.

THE GREAT MIGRATION

Meanwhile, conditions were changing in Mexico. Under dictator Porfirio Díaz, who ruled the country from 1876 to 1880 and again from 1884 to 1911, the economy expanded. Díaz attracted investors from the United States and Great Britain, who poured millions of dollars into developing copper and silver mines, building railroads, and exploiting Mexico's huge oil deposits. A small number of Mexicans who owned the mines as well as the land where the railroads were built grew wealthy. The vast majority of Mexicans, however, did not benefit at all from the economic changes. They performed the backbreaking work of digging in the mines or building the railroads for very low wages.

As a result, an estimated one million Mexicans left Mexico to look for better jobs in the United States. In a mass movement called the Great Migration, they moved to New Mexico, Arizona, California, and other states between 1900 and 1930. Among the immigrants were Juan Fernandez's parents. One reason they chose to move to New Mexico was because other Hispanic families, like Alicia Chavez's parents, were already living there. There was a thriving Hispanic community for new immigrants to join, where they felt accepted.

Juan Fernandez left school early to work in the coal mines of New Mexico. Coal was a vital source of fuel, used by millions of Americans to heat their homes. A coal miner's job was very dangerous. Early in the morning he descended into the darkness of the mine, which was lit only by oil lamps. Underneath the earth, the miner dug coal that was loaded into carts and carried up to the surface. Years of coal mining and breathing coal dust damaged a miner's lungs. If a mine collapsed, a miner might be trapped beneath the surface and severely injured or even killed.

In the Southwest, Mexican miners like Juan Fernandez also faced discrimination. White Americans, known as Anglos, looked down on Mexicans. Mexican miners were paid lower wages than the Anglos. In addition, Mexican miners who lived in the mining towns were segregated from whites and forced to live in run-down areas.

Juan Fernandez could not earn enough from coal mining to support his family, which included Dolores and her two brothers, Marshall and John. Therefore, he also took a job as a farmworker. Throughout the Southwest, many Mexicans worked on large cotton plantations. When they were not picking cotton, these workers migrated north to find other work. Known as migrant farmworkers, they went to Colorado or Nebraska and harvested sugar beets. Juan Fernandez joined these workers, often living in tent camps near the fields. Because they lived in camps, they were called *campesinos*. Other campesinos went north from Colorado to pick potatoes in Idaho, berries in Oregon, or grapes in California.

Migrants like Juan Fernandez often worked for a contractor, known as a *contratista*. The contratista received a specified amount of money from a large farmer, and, in turn, used some of it to pay the migrants to harvest crops. Generally, the contratistas paid the migrants very low wages, keeping as much profit as they could for themselves. Juan Fernandez worked for the contratistas, and he regularly traveled far from home.

Dolores described her father as "charismatic, intelligent, [and] handsome."[11] Despite his good qualities, over time a rift developed between Dolores's mother and father, which may have been increased by his frequent absences as a migrant farmworker. The couple divorced in 1936, and Alicia Fernandez moved with her three children to Stockton, California.

GROWING UP IN STOCKTON

During the 1930s, the United States was mired in the Great Depression. Approximately 25 percent of the population was unemployed. At that time, the government did not provide unemployment benefits to people who were out of work while they looked for new jobs. Instead, charitable institutions, such as local churches, tried to help the unemployed obtain food and clothing. Because so many people were out of work, these charitable agencies were strained past the breaking point.

Many Americans believed that they were being forced to compete with Mexican immigrants for scarce charitable donations and even scarcer jobs. In addition, the immigrants themselves realized that the Depression-era United States no longer offered the same job opportunities that had existed in the past. During the 1930s, approximately 400,000 Mexican immigrants left the United States to return to Mexico. Those who remained faced discrimination.

Dolores's family remained in Stockton, where Alicia Fernandez found a job at a local cannery. The workers there canned fruits and vegetables that were grown in the area for shipment to other parts of the country. Alicia was fortunate to get the job, because there was so much competition for so little work. Many Americans who had lost their farms during the Great Depression traveled west, hoping to find work in the canneries or as migrant workers. They pushed out many Mexican Americans who had done this work in the past. However, the pay at the cannery was low. Alicia Fernandez had to take a second job as a waitress in a local restaurant. While she was working, Alicia left Dolores and her two brothers, Marshall and John, in the care of their grandfather. "My grandfather used to call me 'seven tongues,'" Dolores once said, "because I always talked so much."[12]

Dolores grew up in a neighborhood that was home to people of many different nationalities, including Japanese and Jews. Despite the diversity, she often faced discrimination from the Anglo community. There were signs on restaurants and public swimming pools that said, "No Mexicans Allowed." Dolores's mother was not willing to let discrimination stand in the way of her ambition. She eventually saved enough money to open her own restaurant. She married a man named James Richards, and together they opened a hotel. "My mother was a businesswoman and a wonderful, gentle person," Dolores later recalled. "She always encouraged me to get involved. I was a Girl Scout from ages 8 to 18, so part of my activism started when I was very young."[13]

In 1941, the United States entered World War II. In the Pacific Theater, U.S. troops fought the armies of Japan; in Europe, American soldiers fought the German Nazi armies. Meanwhile, in Stockton, Dolores sold war bonds to help the United States pay for the war effort. In fact, she sold more bonds than any other student in her school. She was supposed to receive a special trophy for her work, but she never got it. "They could not face the fact that a Mexican-American girl had sold the most,"[14] she recalled.

COMING OF AGE IN THE 1940s

During World War II, racial tension broke out between Mexican Americans and Anglos in Los Angeles, south of Stockton. As American involvement in World War II increased, more and more people were joining the armed forces. As a result, jobs opened up for young Mexican immigrants, who were not required to serve in the armed forces. These immigrant workers were resented by young American men who were serving in the war. In 1943, a riot broke out between soldiers who were being trained at military bases around Los Angeles and young Mexican Americans. The soldiers beat up a number of Mexican immigrants. Finally, the U.S. soldiers were forced by their military commanders to leave Los Angeles and return to their bases.

Many of the immigrants entering the United States came as part of the new Bracero Program, started by the Mexican and U.S. governments in 1942. *Braceros*—people who work with their arms—was a term used to refer to Mexican immigrant agricultural workers. There was an enormous demand for agricultural workers during World War II. Many Americans had left the farms to join the armed forces. Others went into defense industries, making airplanes and weapons. President

During World War II, there was a large demand for agricultural workers in the United States, and the U.S. and Mexican governments set up the Bracero Program to meet this demand. Although the program was eliminated in 1964, many migrant farmworkers, such as the ones pictured here, still cross the border from Mexico to the United States each day to look for agricultural work on farms throughout the American Southwest.

Franklin D. Roosevelt signed an agreement—the Bracero Program—with Mexico to recruit Mexican farmworkers and bring them into the United States.

Over the next 22 years, approximately 5 million immigrants crossed the border to work in the United States. Many more wanted to come north, but there were not enough jobs. Mexican recruiters sometimes took bribes from those workers who wanted to be selected for the program. Under the Bracero Program, employers were supposed to pay for the workers' transportation to the fields, food, and housing. However, the food was often of poor quality and the pay was low—about 50 cents an hour. In Stockton, some of the Braceros stayed in

Alicia Fernandez's hotel. Alicia recognized that some were too poor to afford food. She "made sure even her poorest tenants had something to eat."[15] She also let poor migrant workers have a free room in the hotel.

Alicia served as an important role model for Dolores, who learned that a woman could be a successful businessperson while also raising a family. Many Hispanic women were

LUISA MORENO: UNION ORGANIZER

Born in Guatemala in 1906, Luisa Moreno was one of America's first female labor leaders. After spending a brief time in Mexico, where she worked as a journalist and wrote poetry, Moreno moved to New York City with her artist husband in 1928. During the Great Depression, Moreno worked as a sewing machine operator in a Harlem sweatshop, where she founded *La Liga de Costureras*, a Latina garment-workers' union. In 1935, the American Federation of Labor hired her as a professional organizer and she moved to Florida, where she helped African-American and Latina cigar rollers form a union.

Shortly thereafter, in 1938, she joined the Congress of Industrial Organizations (CIO) and served as an international representative and vice president of the United Cannery, Agricultural, Packing, and Allied Workers of America (UCA-PAWA). The following year, she organized *El Congreso Nacional del Pueblo de Habla Hispana* (The National Congress of Spanish-Speaking Peoples), which was the first national organization that brought together Hispanic workers from diverse ethnic backgrounds.

During the late 1930s and 1940s, Moreno lived in California and recruited women to join the UCAPAWA. She helped women workers achieve higher wages and the same pay as men for equal work. Decades later, Dolores Huerta would follow in Moreno's footsteps as a leading female union organizer and inspiration to Hispanics.

mothers and wives. However, their husbands generally believed that a woman's place was in the home, not in the workplace. Alicia presented a different lifestyle that influenced Dolores greatly when she became an adult.[16]

While growing up in Stockton, Dolores did not lose touch with her father. He had left the mines and gone to college, where he earned a degree. Juan Fernandez had also become a member of the New Mexico state legislature and an active union leader. He believed that unions were essential to helping poor workers, like Mexican Americans, improve their pay and obtain better working conditions.[17] Some unions were active in California. Among them was the United Cannery, Agricultural, Packing, and Allied Workers of America (UCA-PAWA), whose leaders included Dorothy Ray Healy and Luisa Moreno. Dolores would later follow in her father's footsteps and become active in the union movement.

HIGH SCHOOL AND BEYOND

Dolores put her own organizing skills to work while she attended high school. She helped organize a teen center. The center was later closed by the local police, however, apparently because they did not want Anglo teens mixing with Mexican Americans and African Americans. "It was terrible," Huerta later said. "I just blacked the whole thing out."[18] After graduating from high school, Dolores decided to go to Stockton College. At the time, very few Latinas (Hispanic women) went on to higher education. She did not finish her degree. Dolores left Stockton to marry Ralph Head when she was nineteen. In the early years of their marriage, the couple had two daughters, Celeste and Lori. Unfortunately, conflicts began to develop between Dolores and Ralph. They gradually grew further and further apart, eventually divorcing in the early 1950s.

After the divorce, Dolores held several different jobs. Her mother helped care for her two children. However, Dolores found none of her jobs very satisfying, and she eventually returned to college for a bachelor's degree and a teaching certificate. In the early 1950s, she started a new career as a teacher. Many of her students came from poor migrant families. "I couldn't stand seeing kids come to class hungry and needing shoes," she said. "I thought I could do more organizing farmworkers than by trying to teach their hungry children."[19]

After less than a year, Dolores Huerta left teaching for a new career that she continued to pursue for more than five decades—community organizer and union leader.

3

Community Organizing

When Dolores Huerta decided to enter community organizing in the 1950s, she became part of a tradition that had existed among Mexican Americans for more than a century. Partly because of Huerta's work, however, community organizing efforts greatly expanded. To achieve this success, Huerta had to make some enormous sacrifices.

EARLY ORGANIZATIONS

After the Mexican-American War of the 1840s, vast areas of the Southwest and California became part of the United States. Mexicans suddenly found themselves living in an Anglo society. American settlers streamed into Arizona, New Mexico, and California. However, many Americans looked down on Mexicans because of their brown skin and their Spanish culture. Mexicans faced severe prejudice, and some became victims of violence at the hands of Anglo settlers.

Mexican Americans often withdrew from Anglo society because they were discriminated against by whites, who looked down on them. Pictured here is a group of Mexican sugarbeet workers in the American Southwest in 1915.

To protect themselves, Mexican Americans often withdrew from Anglo society. They lived in their own neighborhoods, called *barrios*. They also formed *mutualistas*—mutual aid societies. The mutualistas opened schools, because Mexican-American children often faced discrimination in Anglo schools. Mutualistas provided loans to Mexican-American farmers and store owners, and started Spanish newspapers that the residents of the barrios could read in their own language.

Community organizations in the barrios expanded during the twentieth century. Among the best-known organizations was the League of United Latin American Citizens (LULAC). Founded in Corpus Christi, Texas, in 1929, LULAC was led by Ben Garza. Together with the other members of the organization, Garza developed the slogan "All for One and One for All." LULAC campaigned to end the discrimination against Mexican

Americans that existed in many parts of the United States. In many places, Mexican children were required to attend segregated schools—that is, they were educated in separate facilities from white children. The teachers were often second-rate and the buildings were falling down. Mexican Americans, whose families had lived in the United States for generations, were not able to vote. Generally, they were required to pay a poll tax to vote, and many were too poor to afford it.

During the 1940s, LULAC brought lawsuits before the courts that helped end school segregation in Texas. At the same time, LULAC worked to stop segregation in many California schools. The organization brought forth two cases in 1945 and 1946 that ended school segregation in California.

In addition to LULAC, there were labor unions that tried to help Mexican Americans. Union organizing had begun during the nineteenth century among workers in manufacturing. By the mid-twentieth century, large unions like the American Federation of Labor (AFL) had organized thousands of factory workers. The International Longshore and Warehouse Union enlisted many members among the dockworkers in America's ports. Union leaders used strikes and other techniques to obtain better wages and working conditions for their members. A few of these leaders were Mexican Americans. The president of one of the Longshore Union's branches was Bert Corona.

Corona was born in 1918 in El Paso, Texas. His father had fought in the Mexican Revolution, riding with one of its most famous leaders, Pancho Villa. Educated at the University of Southern California, Corona went to work for the Longshore Union in the 1930s. However, he never lost sight of the problems that confronted Mexican Americans. As one of Corona's friends, Nativo Lopez, put it, "Bert saw Mexicanos in the United States, not just as a people suffering racial and national discrimination, but as a working-class community, exploited for their labor. He believed that change would come about by creating organization and leaders among grassroots people, in unions and in the neighborhoods."[20]

Bert Corona was a community leader who worked tirelessly to end the Bracero Program. Under this program, the large farm owners negotiated with the Mexican government for the salaries that they were willing to pay the Braceros. These salaries were very low. As a result, Mexican-American farmworkers who lived in the United States and needed higher wages to support their families were at a great disadvantage. They either had to accept lower wages or lose their jobs. If they tried to form unions and strike for higher wages, they would be fired. As historian J. Craig Jenkins has written: "The growers would simply order up a new crew of braceros and . . . they would finish out the harvest. And when the season was over, the braceros were simply shipped home to Mexico."[21] Corona recognized that the only solution was to stop the Bracero Program and organize Mexican Americans and former Braceros into a powerful union. This would force the large farm owners to pay adequate wages.

CÉSAR CHÁVEZ

Bert Corona was a friend of another community leader, César Chávez. Indeed, Corona helped pave the way for the work that Chávez and Dolores Huerta would later do with the NFWA.

Born in Yuma, Arizona, in 1927, Chávez was three years older than Huerta. Like Huerta's grandfather, Chávez's grandfather Cesario had left Mexico to find a better life in the United States. He bought a farm and raised a family there. One of his sons was Chávez's father, Librado Chávez. Librado and his wife, Juana, divided their time between the farm and running several small businesses, including a general store and a pool hall. However, they lost these businesses during the Great Depression. Librado had given credit to many friends and customers who were hard-pressed for money, and when they could not pay, he had to shut down his businesses.

During the early 1930s, the Chávezes also lost their farm. Severe droughts reduced the size of their crops, forcing them to try to borrow money from the local bank. "But the guy next to us who wanted to get the land was the president of the bank, so the loan was blocked," César Chávez recalled. The Chávez family packed up as much as they could fit in their car and were forced to leave by the deputy sheriff. Chávez later explained, "He had the papers and told us we had to leave or go to jail. My mother came out of the house crying, we children knew there was trouble, but we were confused, worried. For two or three days, the deputy came back, every day. . . . And we had to leave."[22]

Chávez and his family traveled to California, where they became migrant farmworkers. They went from farm to farm across the state, picking a variety of crops, such as tomatoes, melons, and berries. Once a crop was harvested at a large farm, the Chávez family and other migrants had to move to another farm to find more work. The Chávezes were exploited by contractors, known as *coyotes*, who paid them meager wages and sometimes ran off without paying them at all. As Chávez's sister Rita recalled, "We had never worked for anybody else. We never lived away from our home. Here we come to California, and we were lucky we got a tent. Most of the time we were living under a tree, with just a canvas on top of us."[23]

Farmworkers tried to protest the low wages and poor housing conditions. There were strikes in the fields, and some workers simply walked off the job when they felt abused. As Chávez recalled, "Once . . . we were picking cotton when another farmworker started arguing he was being shortchanged in weight. [The workers were paid by the weight in cotton that they picked.] We argued for the worker, and when he quit, we quit too. We quit many jobs over such arguments. . . . We would leave and try to take as many people as we could and go work elsewhere."[24]

Chávez and his brother Richard faced discrimination, much like what Dolores Huerta had encountered. They were forced to sit in classrooms set aside for Mexicans only. "There were lots of racist remarks [from Anglo children] that still hurt my ears when I think of them. And we couldn't do anything except sit there and take it,"[25] Chávez recalled. Richard and César tried to earn extra money by shining shoes along the streets of the towns where their family lived. Once, when they had earned some money, César and Richard went to a restaurant and ordered a hamburger. They did not realize that a sign at one side of the restaurant said, "Whites Only." When they tried to order hamburgers, the waitress was furious with them. "What's the matter, you dumb Mex—can't you read?"[26] she said.

Chávez dropped out of high school and went to work full-time in the fields picking fruits and vegetables. In Delano, an agricultural community, Chávez met a young woman named Helen Fabela at a soda shop. They were married in 1948, and eventually moved to a poor barrio called *Sal Si Puedes* ("Escape If You Can"), in San Jose, California. César and Richard, who lived in a house nearby, worked at a lumber mill. While living in San Jose, Chávez became friendly with a local priest named Father Donald McDonnell. Father McDonnell was visiting the migrant camps, talking about spiritual issues and urging the workers to organize against the farm owners. Chávez, a devout Catholic, accompanied Father McDonnell and talked to the workers, too.

In the early 1950s, Father McDonnell was contacted by the Community Service Organization (CSO), which was also trying to organize farmworkers. Formed in the late 1940s, the CSO focused its efforts on registering Mexican Americans to vote. Many Mexican Americans had lived in the United States for generations but did not vote in U.S. elections. The CSO believed that if Mexican Americans were mobilized to vote and then elected their own candidates to local government in California, new laws could be passed that would improve the lives of the farmworkers.

Father McDonnell told one of the CSO organizers, Fred Ross, about César Chávez. At first, Chávez was skeptical that the CSO or any other organization could help the migrant farmworkers, but eventually Ross won him over. Chávez went

César Chávez and Fred Ross lent their support to the Agricultural Workers Association, of which Dolores Huerta was a member. Ross and Chávez are pictured here during a protest of Dole products in February 1982.

to work for the CSO at a salary of $35 per week. He began to register Mexican Americans to vote so they could help change the laws in California.

It was a difficult task, because the workers were afraid of the huge farm owners who had the power to fire them. In addition, Chávez had to deal with accusations that he was a Communist. During the 1950s, the United States was in the grip of a movement known as McCarthyism. It was named after Senator Joseph McCarthy of Wisconsin. McCarthy convinced many people that various departments of government, labor unions, and even Hollywood film studios were infested with Communists who were trying to undermine the United States. Chávez was accused of being a Communist because he was trying to change the lives and treatment of Mexican Americans. He denied the charges and was able to convince

FRED ROSS

Born in 1910, Fred Ross attended the University of Southern California during the 1930s and wanted to become a teacher, like Dolores Huerta. When no jobs were available, he went to work for the federal government supervising a camp of migrant workers brought north under the Bracero Program. Ross realized that the lives of the migrants had to be improved, and he encouraged them to organize and demand improvements from farm owners. Ross called himself "a social arsonist who goes around setting people on fire."* During the 1940s, Ross helped found the Community Service Organization (CSO) along with Antonio Rios and Edward Roybal. He organized Mexican-American voters and helped elect Roybal to the Los Angeles City Council in 1949.

In 1952, Ross arranged a meeting with César Chávez. At first, Chávez tried to avoid Ross. Chávez did not expect very much from Ross, but he found himself listening as Ross described the role that the CSO had played in an incident called Bloody Christmas. In 1951, the Los Angeles police had beaten up a group of young Mexican Americans. The CSO put enough pressure on the police department to have the officers arrested for brutality. After the meeting with Chávez, Ross wrote, "I think I've found the guy I'm looking for." Chávez later said, "My suspicions were erased. As time went on, Fred became sort of my hero. I saw him organize, and I wanted to learn."** Chávez went to work with Ross in 1952. They spent many years together, and Ross later helped Chávez form the United Farm Workers Association. Ross eventually left the union and became a professor at Syracuse University, where he taught students the principles of community organizing. He died in 1992.

* Dick Meister, "Labor, and a Whole Lot More: A Trailblazing Organizer's Organizer." Available online at *http://www.dickmeister.com/id73.html.*

** Richard Griswold Del Castillo and Richard Garcia, *Cesar Chavez, A Triumph of the Spirit* (Norman, Okla.: University of Oklahoma Press, 1995), 25.

farmworkers that he was simply interested in helping them achieve more power for themselves.

Meanwhile, Chávez was also trying to bring an end to the Bracero Program. He was certain that efforts to organize Mexican-American workers would never help people if the big farm owners had a ready supply of cheap labor available among the Braceros. Because profits on fruits and vegetables are not very high, growers want to keep their costs as low as possible. Instead of hiring local workers, they hired much cheaper Braceros. The large growers also worked together to control prices. They formed cooperatives—groups that decided how much to charge for particular products, such as oranges.

César Chávez realized that the Mexican-American farmworkers were being exploited by the large growers. He wanted to change this situation. As historians Richard Griswold Del Castillo and Richard Garcia wrote,

> Chávez got CSO and community members to apply for work every day [from local growers] . . . and compiled records of their applications and rejections. Next the CSO organized a boycott of local merchants [who bought fruits and vegetables from the growers] to protest their support of the system and to pressure them to change it. Then César organized sit-down strikes in the fields to challenge the hiring of braceros.[27]

CSO AND DOLORES HUERTA

Fred Ross recruited not only César Chávez to the CSO, but also Dolores Huerta. As she said when Ross asked her to join the CSO, "This was, of course, something I had been looking for all my life. When Fred showed us pictures of people in Los Angeles that had come together . . . that had built health clinics, that had gotten people elected to office, I just felt like I had found a pot of gold! If organizing could make this happen, then this is definitely something that I wanted to be part of."[28]

In 1956, Huerta joined a branch of the CSO in Stockton, California. "I had students who didn't have proper clothing or shoes because of the poor wages their parents made,"[29] she said. Huerta decided that her future was not in teaching but in community organizing. She began as a volunteer and eventually became a paid member of the CSO. Some of the teachers who worked with Huerta thought that she was making a mistake when she joined the CSO. She left a secure, paying job for a volunteer position. "The other teachers that I worked with thought I was crazy," she said. "Later on, though, they thought it was wonderful."[30]

During the late 1950s, Huerta's work for the CSO took her from one house to another as she tried to register Mexican Americans to vote. Shortly after joining the CSO, she met César Chávez. "I had heard a lot about him from Fred Ross— César this and César that—but I didn't really get a chance to talk to him the first time I met him, and he didn't make much of an impression on me. . . . I knew he was a great organizer, but he never showed it; it came out in the reports. He was very unassuming."[31]

Meanwhile, Huerta was also working with the Agricultural Workers Association. This group had been started in 1958 by Father Thomas McCullough, a Catholic priest. He received assistance from César Chávez and Fred Ross at the CSO. Huerta eventually became treasurer of the association, which held meetings in the homes of Mexican Americans and soon signed up some of these families as members. The association offered members a credit union where they could borrow money. In addition, the organization offered English classes to Mexican Americans. They needed to understand English to register to vote. Huerta worked hard for the association, although Father McCullough had told her that "farm-labor organizing was no place for a woman."[32]

At the same time, Huerta was trying to enlist support from large unions in an effort to help the farmworkers. She spoke to the AFL-CIO. (By this time, the AFL had merged with another union, the Congress of Industrial Organizations, or CIO.) In 1959, the AFL-CIO had established the Agricultural

Workers Organizing Committee (AWOC). Huerta worked for the AWOC in the late 1950s and early 1960s, eventually becoming secretary-treasurer of the organization. She also tried to provide support for the AWOC from the Agricultural Workers Association. The AWOC began organizing strikes in the California fields to protest the Bracero Program and obtain higher wages. Some workers supported the AWOC because the organization did improve pay, but others were not impressed with its efforts.

Huerta soon recognized that most of the AWOC members were white men with no experience working in the fields. The AWOC was not interested in helping Mexican Americans learn English or obtain credit. Its members only wanted to organize strikes for higher wages. These strikes were expensive and they sometimes turned violent. In 1962, the AWOC leaders were sent to jail and the organization ran short of money. New leaders decided to focus on the contractors—the "coyotes"—who hired the workers. These new leaders believed that if they organized the contractors, the AWOC could control the workers. The coyotes joined the AWOC but made no effort to organize the workers. The workers, in turn, had no respect for the coyotes and had no interest in joining the AWOC.

In the meantime, Huerta had married for a second time during the 1950s. She had met Ventura Huerta, her second husband, at the CSO. With her husband, she had five children—Fidel, Emilio, Vincent, Alicia, and Angela. Nevertheless, her organizing work, the AWOC, and the CSO regularly took Huerta away from her family. Her husband believed that she should spend more time raising their children instead of working for the AWOC and CSO. Father McCullough agreed and wanted Huerta to carry out the traditional roles of wife and mother. Huerta received only $5 a week for her work. She had also convinced Ventura to go to work for the AWOC at a very low salary. It was difficult for both of them, living on little money with so many children to support. The couple were divorced in the early 1960s. A bitter dispute broke out between

Huerta and her husband over who should get custody of their children. In the end, they remained with Dolores.

By the early 1960s, Huerta had also left the AWOC to work full time for the CSO. She worked as a lobbyist, or advocate, for Mexican Americans at the California state capital in Sacramento. As a result of her work, the legislature passed a new law granting retirement benefits to Mexican immigrants who had spent most of their lives in the United States.

By this time, César Chávez had decided that the CSO was not using strong enough methods to force the farm owners to recognize the rights of Mexican-American workers. Chávez also recognized that the Bracero Program might be ending during the 1960s. Many members of Congress believed that the program had given the large growers an unfair advantage over small farmers who could not afford to hire workers for their fields. Chávez decided that the time had come to establish an independent, powerful farmworkers' union to force the growers to grant better working conditions.

At the CSO annual convention in 1962, Chávez, who was the executive director of the organization, brought up the idea of forming a union to the members attending the meeting. When they refused to agree to start a union, Chávez resigned his position as executive director. He said, "I was heartbroken. CSO was my home. I wasn't angry when I left—if I had left angry, my anger would have sustained me—but I was homesick for a long time."[33]

Fred Ross and Dolores Huerta were saddened to see Chávez leave the CSO, but they both understood the reasons for his decision. Before long, Huerta would also leave the CSO to join Chávez.

4

Building the Farm Workers Association

After César Chávez left the Community Service Organization, he was offered a job at the AWOC. He turned down the opportunity to start his own organization instead. Dolores Huerta supported Chávez's efforts and eventually she joined Chávez and helped him build his new organization. It was a great risk to take, considering she had seven children and would receive very little salary from Chávez. Huerta, however, believed in what she and Chávez called *La Causa*—the farmworkers' cause.

FIRST DAYS OF A NEW MOVEMENT

Chávez did not refer to his new organization as a union. The word *union* brought to mind the efforts of the AWOC, which had failed to organize the farmworkers. They had concentrated on short-term efforts, especially strikes for higher wages. Many of these strikes were broken up by the large growers. Some of these growers were part of large corporations. They had strong political connections in

Washington, D.C. As a result, the growers could request more Braceros from Mexico to work for them when the strikers refused to pick their crops. Some of the growers also hired armed guards to break up the strikes. Even if the strikes were successful and the workers achieved higher wages, it did not ensure their loyalty to the union. Once a crop was picked, the workers moved on to another farm that was not covered by the new wage agreement. They often lost interest in the union.

Chávez realized that it might take 5 to 10 years to build a union and mount a successful strike. In the meantime, he went door to door in Delano distributing questionnaires. These asked farmworkers what issues were troubling them and what kinds of changes would improve their lives. On weekends, Dolores Huerta came down from her home in Stockton to join Chávez in his door-to-door campaign.

Both Huerta and Chávez realized that organizing the farmworkers would be very difficult, because they included many diverse groups. Some farmworkers lived in large, permanent communities, or *colonias*, like Delano. Others lived in small colonias made up of only a few houses and a general store. Although many farmworkers were Mexican Americans, others were Anglos. The Anglos had originally come to California looking for work during the Great Depression. Generally, the Anglos did not sympathize with the needs of Mexican Americans. In addition to these groups, there were Mexican farmworkers with green cards, which allowed them to become permanent residents of the United States and work in the fields. They were also free to return to Mexico, if they chose. Many of the "green carders" returned to their homes south of the border at night. These "green carders" were usually not interested in joining a union. They were satisfied with the low wages they were receiving, because the money was far more than they could earn in Mexico. In addition to the green carders, there were large numbers of illegal aliens. These Mexican workers crossed the border illegally. Most of them were unwilling to join a union or to participate in a strike for

Two U.S. Border Patrol inspectors search two Mexican laborers who were caught crossing the U.S.–Mexico border. Many Mexican farmworkers traveled to the United States in order to earn higher wages.

fear of being discovered by the U.S. Border Patrol and sent back to Mexico. Finally, there were Braceros, who had steady employment in the fields and saw no benefit in joining a union. All of these groups had to go out on strike together and agree not to work if the effort was going to succeed.

Instead of talking about strikes and unions, Chávez and Huerta met with groups of workers in their homes to talk about their grievances. They called the new organization the Farm Workers Association (FWA). Chávez said it would provide its members with an insurance program to bury any family member who died at an early age from the backbreaking work of picking fruits and vegetables. The association also planned to start a credit union, from which members could borrow money, and a gasoline cooperative. This co-op, as it was called, would be owned and operated by the members, and prices would be lower than at local gas stations.

This organizing approach was similar to the method used by the CSO. Both Chávez and Huerta had gone door to door recruiting CSO members. They held meetings in members' homes, hoping to sign up more recruits for the CSO. In the early 1960s, Chávez and Huerta built relationships with local farmworkers around Delano. These relationships formed the foundation for what they eventually hoped would become a union. The approach used by Huerta and Chávez also built on the old mutualistas that had helped Mexican Americans in the past. These organizations had offered loans and other forms of assistance to Mexican immigrants. According to historian J. Craig Jenkins, "The Association [founded by Chávez and Huerta] also held festivals and parades on religious and civic holidays and used Catholic and Mexican symbols to stir the workers."[34] These appealed to the workers' pride in their heritage and their strong Catholic religious beliefs.

Chávez charged members of his organization dues of $3.50 per month. This was a large amount of money for workers who were earning only about $1 an hour. However, Chávez believed that, "If things are done with sacrifice, they are more lasting. If they cost more, then we will value them more."[35]

THE FIRST CONVENTION

In 1962, the FWA held its first convention in Fresno, California. About 300 families had already joined the organization, and approximately 250 people came to the convention. To pay for the convention hall, Chávez and Huerta collected contributions from the members as they arrived.

At the convention, the organization officially adopted the name "Farm Workers Association." Chávez and Huerta appeared at the front of the hall to address the members, who voted to campaign for a minimum wage of $1.50 per hour. The members also adopted a flag for the new organization. It was a black eagle in a white circle, on a red background. The eagle was a symbol of the Aztec Indians, the powerful tribe that controlled a large empire in Mexico from the fourteenth to sixteenth centuries.

In the constitution drawn up by the FWA were the words, "Rich men and masters should remember this—that to exercise pressure for the sake of gain upon the indigent and destitute, and to make one's profit out of the need of another, is condemned by all laws, human and divine. To defraud anyone of wages that are his due is a crime which cries to the avenging anger of heaven."[36]

In 1962, Dolores Huerta was still living in Stockton and working part time for the FWA. She was not quite ready to leave her job with the CSO. "I am not quite the long-suffering type," she wrote to Chávez. Nevertheless, she was just scraping by, with the help of child-support payments from her ex-husband, Ventura. "If I can make it through August," she added, "and I know the Good Lord will not let us starve, then in September I can apply for my substitute teacher credential. . . . Until next time, *Viva la Causa*."[37] Despite the hardship she was facing, she continued to drive down to the Delano area, but she asked Chávez to give her money to pay for gas.

During this time, the FWA was steadily growing. By 1964, it had more than 1,000 members. The FWA also had a credit union that could loan small amounts of money to its members. In addition, the FWA was receiving support from powerful religious organizations. The National Council of Churches—a group of American Christian churches—had established a migrant ministry during the 1930s. This organization established schools for the children of migrant workers and provided food and health care. Under the direction of Reverend Chris Hartmire, the migrant ministry became more involved in community organizing during the early 1960s. Hartmire sent two members of the ministry, Reverend Jim Drake and Reverend David Hazen, to help the FWA. Thus, the association gained new staff members paid for by the migrant ministry.

Despite the financial risks and the time she would have to spend away from her family, Dolores Huerta went to work full time for César Chávez when he started his own labor union.

Meanwhile, in 1964, Dolores Huerta made the decision to leave the CSO and join the Farm Workers Association full time. As César Chávez told her, "You have to leave your job. You can't work for a living and fight. You've got to do one or the other. You've got to do this full-time."[38]

"When I made the decision to do it, somebody left a big box of groceries on my front porch in Stockton, and I thought that was just like a sign to me," Huerta recalled. "I knew what it was like to send my kids to school with shoes that had holes. So it was a very, very hard time for us. But again, this is what farmworker families go through every day of their lives."[39] Her starting pay was $5 a week. It was all that the FWA could afford to give her. At first, Huerta and her family lived with the Chávezes in Delano. While she was on the road recruiting members for the FWA, Huerta left her children in the care of Helen Chávez or other friends in the FWA.

FIRST SUCCESSES

President John F. Kennedy, who had started social-activism programs like the Peace Corps, was assassinated late in 1963, but much of his work was continued by the new president, Lyndon Johnson. President Johnson declared a War on Poverty in an effort to help disadvantaged minority groups achieve equality. The FWA received support from "organized labor, several private foundations, the Catholic Church, governmental agencies . . . and several of the other social movements of the period,"[40] according to historian J. Craig Jenkins. For example, a special grant came to the FWA from the Federal Office of Economic Opportunity totaling $260,000 to train members in community organizing.

Meanwhile, the FWA began to publish its own newspaper. It was called *El Macriado, The Voice of the Farm Worker*. One of its writers was Doug Adair, a graduate student who lived in California. Adair had spent some time working in the fields with Mexican farm laborers. He had also experienced the tactics of coyotes who tried to cheat some of the workers out of their money. As a result, Adair left graduate school to join the FWA and write for *El Macriado*. Articles in the newspaper exposed the tactics of unscrupulous contractors and unfair treatment by growers. Among the most popular features of the newspaper was a cartoon about a poor farmworker named Don Sotaco. "The cartoons were very important because a lot of the farmworkers couldn't read,"[41] according to cartoonist Andy Zermeno. Zermeno used humor to portray the problems of

Don Sotaco, who constantly had to put up with injustices from his employers.

Meanwhile, in real life, serious injustices were occurring among rose workers near Delano. These workers, who grew roses, had just discovered that their company was not going to honor a recent agreement to increase their wages. The workers met with Chávez and explained their grievances against the rose company. Although they were fearful about going on strike, the workers eventually agreed with Chávez that a strike was the only way to force the company to abide by its agreement. The workers included green carders, as well as immigrants from the Philippines and Puerto Rico. They gathered together with Dolores Huerta, who held out a crucifix and asked each man to swear to honor the strike. Huerta knew that if any of the rose workers crossed the picket line and went back to work, the effect of the entire strike would be greatly weakened.

On the day of the strike, Huerta went around to visit the houses of all the workers. When she found out that some of them were actually planning to go to work, she prevented them from getting out of the driveway by blocking it with her truck. Despite her efforts, the flower company brought in strike-breakers, and the green carders decided to go back to work. The other workers became very angry. Dolores called the Mexicans traitors to the labor movement. The Mexicans said, "We are Mexican citizens. This isn't our fight."[42]

Meanwhile, another strike had broken out at a migrant worker camp. Workers were being asked to pay much higher rents than they could afford. As a result, they went on strike, helped by the FWA. This strike had barely begun before the FWA became involved in something much larger. This was the strike of the Filipino grape workers around Delano. At first, the strike was led by the AWOC. Chávez and Huerta were unsure whether the FWA was ready to become involved in a large grape strike. A strike would signal that the FWA had become a union, and Chávez had hoped to wait several more years before taking this step. Nevertheless, Chávez sent Huerta to walk the picket line and find out what she could do to help the grape workers.

As the strike grew, Chávez and Huerta realized that they might have to seize the opportunity and become involved. Otherwise, the FWA might lose its support among the farmworkers. They called a meeting of the FWA to discuss whether their members should join the Filipino workers. The meeting was held on September 16, 1965, at Our Lady of Guadalupe Church in Delano. September 16 was Mexican Independence Day, and Our Lady of Guadalupe was the patron saint of Mexico. Chávez and Huerta wanted to emphasize the ties between the FWA and the history of Mexico. This gave the movement more power and acted as a strong bond to bring the workers together.

The church was crowded with FWA members who had come to hear Chávez and Huerta speak. "We are engaged in another struggle for the freedom and dignity which poverty denies us,"[43] Chávez told the crowd. Finally, the FWA members voted. They decided overwhelmingly to join the Filipino strikers. The FWA would strike against the farms where its members worked and refuse to return to work until the growers gave them the same deal that the Filipinos were demanding.

Eventually, the FWA decided to merge with the AWOC to become the United Farm Workers Organizing Committee (UFWOC.) Led by César Chávez and Dolores Huerta, the UFWOC forced the large grape growers to recognize the organization and sign contracts that protected farmworkers and promised them a decent wage.

5

Fighting the Teamsters Union

Among the farmworkers, Dolores Huerta was known as *La Pasionaria* ("The Passionate One"). While most Mexican-American women played traditional roles as wives and mothers, Huerta wanted something different for herself. She became a skilled organizer and union negotiator. She used these skills to lead the grape boycotts and win fair contracts with the grape growers around Delano during the late 1960s. Her skills also became critically important to the UFWOC as it struggled during the early 1970s to defeat the Teamsters Union.

A UNIQUE ROLE

Members of the UFWOC could not help but contrast Dolores Huerta with Helen Chávez, César's wife. Helen played the traditional role of wife and mother, remaining in the background to raise the Chávez children while her husband led the union movement. However, Huerta had grown up in an environment where her

Dolores Huerta felt comfortable being both a mother and a committed social activist in part because her own mother had been a successful working woman, which was unusual for her time.

mother was a different type of role model. Alicia Fernandez had run a hotel while raising her family. She had been a working mother, and Huerta felt comfortable following in her footsteps. While she was married to her second husband, Ventura Huerta, Dolores refused to let the union take second place to her family. This was a major issue that led to their divorce.

Although Huerta always had the support of her mother, others criticized her for what she did. As historian Margaret

Rose put it, "Huerta's union activism is atypical [unusual]. She rebelled against the conventional constraints upon women's full participation in trade union activism, competing directly with male colleagues."[44] Some union leaders resented her for it. Bert Corona, for example, thought she was "too aggressive."[45]

Huerta defined a unique role for herself in an era before the women's movement had begun. Later, during the 1970s, many women began to discard the traditional roles of house-wives and mothers to enter the workplace. There, these women, called feminists, demanded equality with men in terms of pay and leadership positions. Huerta achieved a lead-ership role in the UFWOC long before the feminist movement began.

Huerta's mother had always told Huerta, "Be yourself." From Huerta's viewpoint, she was fulfilling her own sense of self, her own concept of who she was, by working with César Chávez to lead the UFWOC. As Luis Valdez, the founder of Teatro Campesino, explained, "Dolores was a 35-year-old fire-brand in 1965, and she was commanding crusty macho [strong and manly] campesinos 20 years her senior. . . . She was a woman, a Mexican American, a Chicana [Hispanic woman] cutting a swath of revolutionary action across [California]."[46] In her role as a union leader, Huerta regularly put in 18-hour days organizing boycotts, walking picket lines, and negotiating with growers for new contracts.

THE BATTLE BEGINS WITH THE TEAMSTERS

While Huerta was involved in negotiations with the grape growers around Delano in 1970, the UFWOC received word that trouble was brewing elsewhere in California. Lettuce and other vegetable growers were afraid of the growing power of the UFWOC. About 90 percent of all iceberg lettuce was grown in the Salinas Valley, south of San Francisco. Instead of dealing with the UFWOC, the growers signed agreements with the Teamsters Union.

The Teamsters were primarily a union of truck drivers, but they had also unionized workers in fruit and vegetable packing plants. Unlike the UFWOC, the Teamsters were prepared to work closely with the large growers. The growers agreed to give the Teamsters wage increases for the farmworkers they organized. In return, the Teamsters agreed that they would cooperate with the growers and not set up grievance committees. These committees, made up of union members at each large farm, listened to complaints from farmworkers if the growers tried to treat them unfairly.

In addition, the growers did not want hiring halls on each farm. Union leaders used the hiring halls to organize their members. According to historian J. Craig Jenkins, the UFWOC "used the hiring halls to collect dues, recruit pickets, organize solidarity events, and deliver services as well as make sure that priority jobs went to loyal supporters. The growers, of course, preferred their own hiring and . . . the continued use of labor contractors."[47] The Teamsters were prepared to go along with the growers and work with the contractors. The contractors gathered together laborers to work in each field and paid them with money from the growers. As a result, the contractors had a very powerful position in the agricultural community. The Teamsters were willing to cooperate with the contractors and, through them, control the laborers.

While Dolores Huerta continued to negotiate with the grape growers, César Chávez went to Salinas to protest the agreement between the Teamsters and the large vegetable growers. He met with hundreds of workers and their families who did not want to become members of the Teamsters Union. They decided to go on strike. At the same time, Chávez and Huerta planned to announce another boycott. This tactic had worked with the grape growers; perhaps it might also work with vegetable and fruit growers.

Negotiations began between the UFWOC and the Teamsters in 1970. Chávez and Huerta met with the Teamster leaders, but there was very little trust between the two sides.

Eventually, both unions agreed to accept help from the Catholic Bishops' Committee. Some of the bishops supported the UFWOC. As a result, the UFWOC agreed to call off the strikes for 10 days. Chávez made it clear, however, that he expected the growers to begin negotiating with the UFWOC during the 10-day period.

However, the growers showed no willingness to negotiate. The UFWOC members wanted to go back on strike before the 10-day period was over. At a noisy meeting, Dolores Huerta addressed the workers and read a message from Chávez who could not attend the meeting. "The only thing we have to lose by waiting is our chains,"[48] the letter said. In other words, he wanted the workers to be patient, to wait out the 10 days as they had agreed, and then go on strike if necessary. But when the growers decided to keep their contracts with the Teamsters, the UFWOC membership voted to strike.

The strikers faced a violent reception from the Teamsters, who called in "goon squads." These were people paid by the Teamsters to beat up the strikers. Meanwhile, in 1970, Dolores Huerta began leading a lettuce boycott against the Robert Antle Company. Antle was the largest grower of lettuce in the Salinas Valley and sold its lettuce in California and other parts of the United States. Huerta received assistance from Fred Ross, her old boss at the Community Service Organization. Ross often worked as an advisor in the union organizing effort.

At the same time, a boycott had also been started by the UFWOC against another large lettuce grower, InterHarvest. This grower was owned by the powerful United Fruit Company, producer of Chiquita bananas. United Fruit was afraid that a boycott would hurt the sales of its profitable Chiquita brand. As a result, the company agreed to give up its contract with the Teamsters and negotiate with the UFWOC.

Dolores Huerta negotiated with the company's representative, Will Lauer, through long, agonizing bargaining sessions that lasted far into the night.

As the company slowly began to agree to consider a higher wage for its farmworkers, Lauer said, "I truthfully don't understand where we're going." Huerta told him, "We're going for a better way of life for the farmworkers." At one point, Lauer admitted that he wanted to come to an agreement with the union in part because his two young sons were ardent supporters of the UFWOC.[49] Eventually, Huerta achieved an agreement that boosted workers' hourly pay by 35 cents to $2.10.

Shortly afterward, several other large growers decided to give up their Teamster contracts and negotiate with the UFWOC. They included Pic N Pac, as well as Fresh Pict, which was owned by the Purex Company. Purex was a manufacturer of well-known cleaning products and was afraid that a boycott might hurt sales of its other non-agricultural products.

THE BATTLE CONTINUES

The Teamsters, however, were not prepared to accept these decisions and do nothing. They brought goon squads to InterHarvest and shut down the farms so InterHarvest could not ship out any lettuce. The UFWOC continued to strike against Antle farms. However, Antle, which had a contract with the Teamsters, received support from the California courts, which ordered the UFWOC to call off the lettuce boycott. When César Chávez refused, he was arrested and put in jail in November 1970. The jailing of Chávez became a huge media event. In December, Ethel Kennedy, the widow of Senator Robert Kennedy and a strong supporter of Chávez, visited César in jail. Chávez was released just before Christmas, and the California Supreme Court ruled that the UFWOC could continue the lettuce boycott.

During 1971, the UFWOC trained more people to participate in the lettuce boycott in major cities across the United States. However, the UFWOC was hampered by a lack of funds to pay the workers. In addition, the Teamsters opposed the boycott. They continued to carry lettuce in their trucks to large

During the late 1960s and 1970s, Dolores Huerta and César Chávez organized boycotts on such agricultural products as grapes. Pictured here are picketers outside an Oakland, California, supermarket who are urging shoppers not to buy grapes.

supermarkets. They also convinced other unions not to support the boycott. For example, the Retail Clerks and Butchers Union, whose members worked in supermarkets, refused to support the UFWOC and stocked lettuce on the produce shelves.

TEAMSTERS AND GRAPE GROWERS

While the UFWOC was dealing with the lettuce growers, a new crisis arose in the grape industry. The union contracts between the UFWOC and the grape pickers were due to expire in April

1973. Before the contracts expired, César Chávez visited the large growers. The growers could decide to continue doing business with the UFWOC or switch to the Teamsters. Chávez asked the growers to renew their contracts with the UFWOC. Each grower assured Chávez that they would sign another contract with the UFWOC. But when the contracts actually expired, the grape growers signed with the Teamsters. Large growers like Gallo threw out the UFWOC without even asking the farmworkers whom they wanted to represent them. Many farmworkers wanted to be represented by the UFWOC, not the Teamsters. Teamsters went into the vineyards, trying to force farmworkers to sign up with the union. Any farmworkers who refused to join the Teamsters were fired from their jobs. Since the Teamsters had the contracts from the large growers for hiring employees, the union controlled who was hired and who was fired. Workers who supported the UFWOC went out on strike and began picketing the grape vineyards to stop the Teamsters.

Violence broke out between the UFWOC and the Teamsters that lasted during the remainder of 1973. The *Wall Street*

VIOLENCE IN THE FIELDS

UFWOC strikers often risked their lives as they battled the Teamsters in 1973. Sixteen-year-old picketer Marta Rodriguez was sprayed with mace by police during the United Farm Workers grape strike at Giumarra vineyards. The police then pushed Rodriguez to the ground, handcuffed her, and took her to jail. Another demonstrator, Frank Valenzuela, was clubbed by police before being handcuffed. Sixty-year-old farmworker Juan de la Cruz was walking a picket line with his wife, Maximina. Suddenly, five shots were fired from a passing car. De la Cruz was hit in the chest and died. Soon afterward, Maximina died, too. In total, 3,500 farmworkers were sent to prison during the violent summer of 1973.

Journal reported that a priest named Father John Bank, who was working with the UFWOC, had stopped at a restaurant for lunch. A member of the Teamsters walked up to Father Bank and punched him in the nose, sending the priest to the hospital.[50] Although Chávez urged his members to practice nonviolence, some of them reacted violently against the Teamsters.

By the end of the year, the UFWOC had lost most of its contracts. Its membership, which had stood at 70,000 in 1970, had dropped by more than 80 percent. The UFWOC finally called off the strike effort, but resorted to grape boycotts to oppose the large growers.

THE STRUGGLE FOR NEW LEGISLATION

In September 1973, the UFWOC held a convention in Fresno. Dolores Huerta and César Chávez sat at a huge table in front of the members, as they adopted a new name for their union. The union would be called the United Farm Workers of America, or the UFW. The union also ratified a new constitution that declared the union's purpose was "to unite under its banner all individuals employed as agricultural laborers, regardless of race, creed, sex or nationality."[51] The UFW prided itself on the benefits offered to its members, including a credit union, low-interest loans, and inexpensive medical care. None of these benefits was offered by the Teamsters. Still, at the end of 1973, the UFW found itself falling way behind the Teamsters in terms of membership. The Teamsters had the power of the huge growers behind them.

All of this gradually began to change in 1974. California voters elected a new governor, Jerry Brown, who was a Democrat and a friend of the UFW. In fact, the UFW had campaigned for his election. Brown replaced the Republican governor Ronald Reagan, who had been a friend of the large growers. The leadership of the UFW recognized that the union could only revive itself if the laws were changed. These laws had to prevent the growers from signing contracts with the Teamsters without fair and open elections by the farmworkers

Union leaders like Dolores Huerta and César Chávez were excited when Democrat Jerry Brown (pictured here) became the governor of California. Brown was a staunch supporter of the United Farm Workers of America.

to decide which union they wanted to join. Chávez and Huerta hoped that Governor Brown would support such laws. Early in 1975, however, as he began his governorship, Brown was not sure that he wanted to go head-to-head with the powerful growers.

César Chávez decided that he needed to convince Governor Brown that the UFW still had some power, too. During the winter, Chávez led a march on the Gallo Vineyards. Gallo had signed an agreement with the Teamsters. The march from San Francisco to Gallo headquarters in Modesto, California, caught the media's attention. It also convinced both Gallo and Governor Brown to consider legislation that might change the existing laws regarding union agreements.

In 1975, Governor Brown and the legislature agreed on a new law, called the Agricultural Labor Relations Act (ALRA). California was only the second state in the country to pass this kind of legislation, after Hawaii. The law protected the Teamsters' contracts for the time being. Then there would be new elections by the farmworkers to choose the union they wanted to represent them. But the big winner was the UFW. Under the new law, the union won the right to secret-ballot elections. The secret ballot meant that the workers could not be forced to join the Teamsters or lose their jobs. They could vote for the UFW, which could then negotiate with the growers. If

SÍ, SE PUEDE

California was not the only state where the United Farm Workers of America (UFW) battled for the rights of farmworkers. In Florida, the union organized workers in the citrus industry who picked oranges and grapefruit. UFW organizers also worked successfully to defeat a law that would have prevented hiring halls for unions. This would have given the growers, rather than the union, power over who was hired or fired. In Arizona, Dolores Huerta campaigned tirelessly to achieve union recognition for workers. In fact, she came up with a slogan that has long been identified with the UFW: *Sí, Se Puede* ("Yes, We Can"). "We'd have a mass [Catholic religious service] every night and a meeting after mass," Huerta recalled. "We were trying to get [more people] to join the mass. . . . One of the fellows said to me, 'In California you can do these things. [But] you can't do this in Arizona.' I said, '*Sí, se puede*.' It stuck."*

* Lu Herrera, "For the Sake of Good," *Hispanic* (May 2003), nos. 28–29.

the growers refused to negotiate, then the union could call a strike. In addition, the law covered not only farmworkers who lived permanently in local communities but migrant workers as well. Therefore, the migrants had a much bigger stake in the union elections. Finally, the law set up an Agricultural Labor Relations Board (ALRB) to ensure that the law was enforced.

ENFORCING THE ALRA

Passing a law was one thing. Enforcing it was something else. The UFW demanded the right to go onto farms to gather support among the workers for the next election. The large growers resisted this idea, threw out the UFW organizers, and let Teamster organizers into the fields. In addition, the growers fired farmworkers who sympathized with the UFW, and brought in other workers to take their place. These actions probably had an impact on the new elections held under the ALRA in 1975. These elections were evenly split between the Teamsters and the UFW.

The ALRB also lacked the money to supervise all the elections, so it was easy for Teamsters and growers to intimidate farmworkers. Many migrants also resented the UFW hiring halls, which gave preference to union members. However, migrants who traveled from farm to farm throughout the state or from one state to another were not interested in union membership. In many of the places that they worked, the laborers were not organized by the UFW or any other union.

During this period, Dolores Huerta helped lead the UFW organizing effort, while also lobbying at the state capitol in Sacramento for more laws to protect farmworkers. One of her major successes was a new law that eliminated the short-handled hoe, known as *el cortito*. Workers were expected to use *el cortito*, or the devil's arm, as it was often called, to weed rows of vegetables. The short hoe, only 24 inches long, required workers to bend over for hours in the fields, causing many of them to rapidly develop severe back problems. Under the law, el cortito was to be replaced with a long-handled hoe.

Dolores Huerta made many influential speeches as she worked to lobby for new laws to protect farmworkers. Her efforts eventually helped lead to some important changes in working conditions.

However, Huerta was less successful in her efforts to win passage of Proposition 14. This proposition would have given the ALRB permanent funding to supervise the new California ALRA and prevent union organizers from being driven out of the fields. Nevertheless, California voters defeated the proposition when it was put on the November election ballot in 1976. The growers convinced a majority of the voters that the UFW organizers were jeopardizing the safety of defenseless growers.

Although Proposition 14 was defeated, the UFW continued to win victories across California. In 1976, approximately 80 percent of the elections were won by the UFW. That is, farmworkers voted to have the UFW, not the Teamsters, represent them in negotiations with the growers. Early the following year, the Teamsters announced that they were pulling out of their effort to organize the farmworkers. Although the Teamsters continued to sign up truck drivers who hauled produce and workers who were employed in packing plants, the UFW had won the battle for the agricultural fields.

6

The Success of the UFW

By the late 1970s, the UFW had signed up 100,000 farmworkers as members of the union. This was quite an achievement for a union that had been created only 15 years earlier. Yet success brought its own problems. Internal conflicts began to affect the union, and Dolores Huerta found herself in the middle of them.

UFW VICTORY

The UFW victory over the Teamsters Union was closely followed by a massive strike in California. In 1979, the UFW confronted the lettuce growers in the Salinas Valley and Imperial Valley, which was located close to the Mexican border. When César Chávez, Dolores Huerta, and their fellow negotiators asked the lettuce growers for a large pay increase and money to help provide medical insurance for the farmworkers, the growers refused. The result was the massive lettuce strike of 1979.

In 1979, the United Farm Workers of America demanded better conditions for the workers who labored in California lettuce fields such as this one in Salinas, California. As a result of the strike and boycott, the UFW was successful in winning a pay raise for farmworkers.

Huerta and Chávez were encouraged by the enormous strength of their union. However, violence broke out along the picket lines. A union striker named Rufino Contreras was killed by rifle fire from guards employed by the growers. Union members struck back and violently attacked scabs who were trying to cross the picket lines.

Supporting the growers was the Ku Klux Klan, which was organizing people in California to break the strike. The Klan had been formed in the South more than a century earlier to protect white people who felt threatened by African Americans. Klan horsemen wearing white sheets and covering their faces with white hoods rode across the South terrorizing African Americans, who had recently been freed from slavery after the Civil War. By the twentieth century, the Klan targeted not only African Americans but also other

DOLORES HUERTA'S LEGACY

LABOR AND CHICANA LEADER

Dolores Huerta has long been considered an outstanding labor leader. Indeed, the California state senate presented her with the Outstanding Labor Leader award in 1984. Nine years later, in 1993, she was inducted into the National Women's Hall of Fame. The Hall of Fame called her one of the twentieth "century's most powerful and respected labor movement leaders."

Huerta has also been a leader of the Chicano/Chicana movement in the United States. Beginning in the 1960s, this movement gained momentum as an effort to recognize the important contributions of Mexican Americans. The movement led to the teaching of courses in Mexican literature at many colleges and universities. Bilingual education in both Spanish and English was offered in public schools. Mexican-American women played a prominent role in the Chicana movement, which became part of the broader American feminist movement. Its goal was to achieve equality for women in all aspects of life.

No Chicana achieved as prominent a role in organized labor as Dolores Huerta. Leading strikers and union pickets, Huerta was arrested more than 20 times. As a community organizer, she was among the first role models for other Chicanas. Huerta was not afraid to fill both the role of wife/mother and union leader. According to authors Richard Griswold del Castillo and Richard Garcia, "Huerta did not consider herself to be a feminist or Chicana leader: she just followed her assumptions that equality is basic to life, and that justice, fairness, is the key."* Although she pushed for equality for women, Huerta realized that men were largely in control of the UFW. But she said, "I know that the history of our union would have been quite different had it not been for my involvement. So I am trying to get more of our women to hang in there. The energy of women is important. . . . The participation of women has helped keep the women nonviolent."**

* Richard Griswold del Castillo and Richard Garcia, *Cesar Chavez, A Triumph of the Spirit* (Norman, Okla.: University of Oklahoma Press, 1995), 71.
** Ibid.

non-white minority groups, including Mexican-American farmworkers.

Although the UFW faced huge obstacles, the union was successful in bringing many of the large growers to the negotiating table. The growers realized that the strikes would continue and their lettuce would never be picked and brought to market. The growers signed new agreements that included higher wages and health-care programs for the workers.

By 1980, the UFW had reached the height of its power. Fully one-third of the more than 300,000 farmworkers in California were members. In addition, the UFW was winning contracts from growers outside California, in states like Florida.

During the 1980s, the UFW won an hourly wage rate for its workers of almost $6 per hour, almost five times more than the workers earned in 1965. Union members also received unemployment insurance when they did not work, as well as paid vacations. Even nonunion workers benefited from the UFW success. These workers received more than $5.50 an hour. Farm owners decided to keep the pay relatively high to prevent workers from wanting to join the UFW.

SUCCESS BRINGS ITS OWN PROBLEMS

Although the UFW had succeeded in defeating the Teamsters and the large growers, other conflicts began to emerge, right inside the UFW. César Chávez had a reputation for being a micromanager. That is, he wanted to keep his eye on everything that was going on in the union and have other leaders consult him about every decision.

While some of his subordinates disagreed with Chávez's management style, they were not strong enough to persuade him to change. Chávez had become a nationally important figure during the grape boycott of the 1970s because of his fasts and his unselfish devotion to the cause of the farmworkers. Chávez believed that all union officials should push themselves unselfishly, working for little or no money, just as he did.

During the early 1980s, Chávez did not want to have to depend on strikes and boycotts to get results. Under the direction of Dolores Huerta, the UFW was running a successful lobbying effort in Sacramento. Huerta was also lobbying for workers' rights in Washington, D.C. Chávez wanted to focus more attention and spend more money on these efforts.

Instead of trying to change Chávez, who had a very strong personality, some of the top UFW officials began to resign. According to historian J. Craig Jenkins, Jerry Cohen, who headed the UFW legal team, left because Chávez refused to pay UFW lawyers an adequate salary. According to Jenkins, Chávez also brought family members into top positions in the union. In response to Chavez's unwillingness to change his policies, leaders like Marshall Ganz, who directed many of the UFW's organizing efforts, resigned in 1981.[52]

Dolores Huerta herself had many disagreements with Chávez. She once stated that,

> César and I have a lot of personal fights, usually over strategy or personalities. I don't think César himself understands why he fights with me. We have these heart-to-heart talks every six months or so on how we're not going to fight anymore, and how demoralizing it is to everybody else that we do. But then, like the next day, we'll have another fight. . . . He says, "I know that I treat you very mean. . ." But I understand it. He knows I might get angry or feel bad about it, but I'm not going to leave the Union.[53]

Huerta did not resign from the UFW. Indeed, she remained Chávez's close colleague while he continued to direct the union. "Totally fearless," he called her, "both mentally and physically." Indeed, she was much like Chávez himself, which may have been why they quarreled regularly. One of the field workers referred to Huerta as "Our Adelita." (Adelita was a Mexican woman who had fought alongside the rebels who overthrew the dictator Porfirio Díaz during the Mexican Revolution.[54]) As a large grower recalled, "You don't get anything from Dolores Huerta unless you fight for it and you earn it. . . . She is vindictive and carries a certain amount of resentment. I wouldn't ever expect anything to be relented [given up] by her."[55]

During the 1980s, Huerta devoted most of her time to the UFW. She helped the union build up its pension plan program for retired workers, health-insurance plans, and housing for poor workers. In addition, she was involved in organizing a union-run Spanish radio station in California called KUFW, or Radio Campesina.

However, Huerta's devotion to the union took a toll on her family. By the 1980s, she had 11 children—seven of them with her two husbands, and four more after she began a relationship with Chávez's brother, Richard. During the 1970s, the couple began living together. Dolores and Richard's children were Juanita, Maria Elena, Ricky, and Camilla. When Huerta was involved in union business, she had to miss important events in the lives of her children. As *Los Angeles Times* writer James Rainey wrote, "She would miss birthdays . . . and school open houses. The children could not help but feel jealous of their mother's first love, the union. But they basked in a feeling that they were a part of history.

"She wasn't ours to have. She sort of belonged to the farmworker movement. And it was our job to support her,"[56] said Emilio [one of her sons].

"Although we weren't a traditional farmworker family whose livelihood depended on harvesting crops, we felt that way. As a labor organizer, my mother had to follow workers in their seasonal patterns, and we traveled around with her. . . . Sometimes we attended as many as three or four different schools in a year,"[57] added Emilio. Huerta's daughter Maria Elena said, "At certain times it was hard having a mom who always worked and wasn't your typical mother. As I get older it becomes easier to understand why those sacrifices were made."[58]

Despite all of her hard work, Huerta was sometimes criticized by other union leaders for working too closely with César Chávez. They believed she should have talked him into loosening his control over the union and broadening the top leadership. When some union members in Salinas disagreed with Chávez, he struck back. He directed Huerta to drive them out of the union. Marshall Ganz blamed her for hurting the union. "I think she exacerbated [increased] César's difficulties,"[59] he said.

UNION DIFFICULTIES

Troubles within the UFW began to grow during the 1980s. One reason was Chávez's decision to change the UFW's emphasis and focus more on removing pesticides from the agricultural fields. Since the 1960s, Chávez and Huerta had campaigned to remove pesticides from the fruit and vegetable fields. Pesticides were used to kill insects that destroyed valuable crops. However, the pesticides also affected farmworkers, causing serious skin rashes, breathing problems, and possibly even cancer.

In 1984, César Chávez announced a new grape boycott. This one was aimed at forcing the large growers to remove dangerous pesticides from the fields. Unlike in the 1960s, however, the boycott had very little impact. The United States had become more conservative, and people were no longer interested in major social reforms. The Republican administration of President Ronald Reagan was pro-business and anti-union. Indeed, while Reagan had been governor of California during the late 1960s, he had been one of the chief opponents of the UFW. Chávez's focus on the grape boycott took valuable resources away from union organizing and strikes. This was one reason why the membership of the UFW began to decline during the 1980s.

Another reason was the political climate in California. Voters had elected a Republican governor, George Deukmejian. The new governor set out to weaken the power of the ALRB. Soon after the ALRB was organized, during the administration of Governor Brown, it supervised more than 400 elections for

In 1984, César Chávez instituted a boycott on grapes to protest the use of toxic pesticides in the growing process. Chávez is pictured here in 1986 at a rally in New York City.

union representation on large California farms. The number of elections supervised by the ALRB declined during the 1980s, as its budget was cut. In addition, the ALRB greatly reduced its investigations of complaints brought by union members into illegal actions by the large growers. There were 1,000 complaints filed each year during the 1970s, but very few were filed in the 1980s. The ALRB ruled that more than 80 percent of those that were filed had no foundation.[60]

Another factor that hurt the UFW was the growing poverty in Mexico, which was driving many more immigrants across the border. During the 1980s, the population of impoverished Mexicans grew by almost one-third. Few new jobs were being created within the Mexican economy. Therefore, many Mexicans came north looking for work. American immigration law only permitted a limited number of legal immigrants to enter the United States. The rest crossed the border illegally. These illegal immigrants were afraid to join a union, go on strike, or draw any attention to themselves. In 1986, due in part to lobbying by Dolores Huerta in Washington, D.C., the federal immigration law was changed by Congress. Any illegal immigrant who had lived in the United States since the beginning of 1982 could become a citizen. In addition, any illegal immigrant who had worked in the United States for at least 90 days between 1985 and 1986 could become a legal immigrant. Finally, the law fined any employers who hired illegals not covered by the new law.

The new law enabled more than 2 million illegal immigrants to achieve legal status in the United States. Even so, many thousands of illegal immigrants continued to cross the border each year. The fines that were supposed to be charged against employers who hired these immigrants were not enforced. As a result, many illegal immigrants were hired by large growers in California. The growers paid these workers only about $3 per hour, far less than the $7 per hour paid to members of the UFW. This cheap source of labor undercut the power of the UFW in contract talks. The growers had also come up with a new method of defeating the union. As reporters Susan Ferriss and Ricardo Sandoval wrote, "The farms could void union contracts if they shut down their operations, then transferred ownership to a third party, usually a relative or a consultant. Many farms reemerged with new names."[61] Union workers were fired, because the new farm owners had not signed contracts with them. Illegal immigrants were hired in their place.

By the late 1980s, UFW membership had declined to about 30,000. To try to revive the UFW and draw attention to the grape boycott, César Chávez began a new fast in 1988. Since Chávez was now in his sixties, Huerta was concerned about his physical ability to undertake such a fast. One of her sons, Dr. Fidel Huerta, monitored Chávez's health. At one point, Dr. Huerta urged Chávez to stop fasting, saying, "There is a need for hospitalization at this point. I have suggested he stop the fast."[62] Chávez received support from several children of the late Senator Robert F. Kennedy, who visited him during the fast. Finally, after 36 days, he ended his fast and celebrated with a Roman Catholic Mass.

Nevertheless, the sad plight of many farmworkers continued. According to a University of California study from the 1980s, the majority of farmworker families were earning only about $9,000 annually—more than $1,500 below the national poverty level. Because farmworkers traveled from farm to farm looking for work, about 90 percent of their children never finished high school.[63] This meant that they were unable to find higher-paying jobs and had little choice but to work in the fields like their parents before them. Although the UFW had achieved substantial gains for some farmworkers, there was still much to be done.

New UFW Leadership

Shortly after César Chávez broke his fast in 1988, Dolores Huerta was in San Francisco. She was picketing a visit by Vice President George H. W. Bush and handing out leaflets about the UFW grape boycott. Police tried to control the protestors and ensure security for Bush, who was campaigning for president of the United States. One of the police struck Huerta with his nightstick, breaking several of her ribs and severely damaging her spleen. She was rushed to the hospital, where doctors worked to save her life. Later, she received a settlement worth $825,000 from the city of San Francisco for being struck by the police. Huerta, who had always lived frugally, joked that she would need to open a bank account to safeguard all this money. Nevertheless, neither her run-in with the police nor her newly found money stopped Huerta from continuing her work on behalf of the UFW.

Dolores Huerta gave up financial security to work with César Chávez in order to win better conditions for farmworkers. However, after a run-in with police in 1988 at a protest against presidential candidate George H. W. Bush, she was awarded a large settlement and joked about her newfound wealth.

UFW AND THE FARMWORKERS

In 1989, César Chávez celebrated his sixty-second birthday. Among the many people who honored Chávez was Dolores Huerta, the first vice president of the UFW.

Although they were celebrating a personal milestone for Chávez, the union continued to struggle. UFW membership had declined, and its power to help the farmworkers had weakened.

Farmworkers like Juan Mendoza had earned as much as $500 a week during the 1980s. By the 1990s, his pay was as little as $200 weekly. On many days he could not find work, because so many illegal immigrants had come across the border to find jobs in the fields. Many of these illegal workers were hired by contractors, who were doing a brisk business in California. In the San Joaquin Valley, contractors hired workers without even telling them how much they were to be paid until after the harvest. Then the contractors took money for bringing the workers to the fields, feeding them lunch, and giving them tools. As a result, a laborer might make $35 for two days of work but by the time the contractor took out his fees, the worker actually owed the contractor $2 at the end of the job.[64]

Most farmworkers could only afford to live in meager housing. Juan Marciel, a typical farmworker, worked in the San Joaquin Valley during the 1990s. He shared a tiny hovel with 12 other people who had no beds. Marciel sent home $200 each month to his wife and children in Mexico. In the fields, workers had toilets, but there was often little or no drinking water. Pay had declined by 10 percent since the 1980s and by as much as 25 percent if the workers were hired by contractors.[65] During the 1990s, a new Republican governor in California, Pete Wilson, proved to be no friendlier toward the UFW than his predecessor, George Deukmejian. This made union organizing extremely difficult.

NEW LIFE FOR THE UFW

Although Chávez and Huerta had been focused on the battle against pesticides instead of organizing workers, Chávez began to redirect his efforts in 1992. He led a battle against a large lettuce company, Bruce Church, Inc. Church and the UFW had been locked in battle since the 1970s. The company refused to sign a new contract with the union, which responded by starting a lettuce boycott. One supermarket chain in California, Lucky Supermarkets, even agreed to stop purchasing Church lettuce. Church sued the UFW, and the legal battle was still going on during the 1990s in California and Arizona, where the company owned many farms.

Chávez traveled to Arizona to lead the fight against Church in 1993. The struggle proved to be too exhausting for him.

César Chávez passed away in 1993 at the age of 66. Pictured here are participants in the César Chávez Memorial March in Detroit, Michigan, which marked the six-year anniversary of the labor leader's death.

Chávez was 66 and had grown weary from so many battles. While he was staying in Arizona, he died in his sleep. Since his mother had lived into her 90s, many members of the UFW had not expected Chávez to die so young. "In a way, we could say that the work took its toll and eventually took him from us, sooner than it should have,"[66] Huerta said. The loss of César Chávez was mourned by many members of the union. Just before his passing, Huerta seemed to know that Chávez was reaching the end of his life. He was much mellower than he had been in the past. "For the last six weeks we hadn't had a single fight,"[67] she said.

Approximately 40,000 people attended Chávez's funeral in La Paz, California, where the UFW headquarters was located. His body was laid out in a simple pine coffin, made by his brother Richard, Dolores Huerta's companion. Well-known political leaders, like the Reverend Jesse Jackson, attended the funeral, along with many farmworkers whom Chávez had helped during the years he ran the UFW. The funeral was also attended by other union leaders, such as Baldemar Velasquez, president of the Farm Labor Organizing Committee in Ohio. His leadership had been inspired by Chávez.

"We must continue *la lucha* [the struggle]," Huerta said after Chávez's death. "We want the world to know that this union has a very strong and very firm foundation."[68]

Although some observers believed that Dolores Huerta might be the next president of the UFW, the leadership passed to Chávez's son-in-law, Arturo Rodriguez. At the age of 43, Rodriguez had spent most of his career working in the union, beginning with the grape boycott of the 1970s.

HUERTA AND RODRIGUEZ

Following Chávez's death, both Huerta and Rodriguez focused their attention on the UFW. "We really spent a lot of time trying to come back together again to determine what was going to happen. And how to continue what we'd inherited and make sure it moved forward into the future. The grower community hoped and believed that with César gone it would be the end of this movement,"[69] Rodriguez said.

To help revive the UFW, Rodriguez led a 24-day march from Delano to Sacramento in 1994. It was similar to a march that had been led by César Chávez in 1975. Thousands of farmworkers joined the march, including many who carried the UFW's red flag with its black eagle symbol. The march was designed to draw attention to the UFW's new focus on union organizing.

Workers responded to the union's efforts. Later in 1994, the UFW won several elections among fruit and vegetable growers that added 1,000 new members to the UFW. This influx of new members was not lost on the growers, who were well aware that this was a major accomplishment for the UFW, and as a spokesman for the growers admitted, "It caught us by surprise."[70] During 1994, the UFW signed up an additional 10,000 members. Rodriguez himself was out in the fields, talking to workers and trying to gather their support. New organizers were assigned by the UFW to meet with workers and persuade them to vote for the union when elections were held at local farms. One of the UFW victories happened at a large farm owned by the powerful Dole Food Company. Dole was so upset that it fired 450 strawberry workers after they voted for the UFW. Dole said, however, that the decision had nothing to do with the UFW victory, that it had been made much earlier. "Harvesting strawberries is no longer profitable,"[71] the company claimed.

Huerta worked alongside Rodriguez in the effort to organize the strawberry workers employed at Dole. Although Huerta was now in her 60s, she directed meetings, led strikers on the picket lines, and trained new union members to recruit workers. Joined by Richard Chávez, she chanted, "Long live the strawberry pickers! Long live César Chávez!"[72]

In 1995, the UFW signed an agreement with the Bear Creek Production Company, the biggest rose grower in the United States. Located in California, it employed 1,400 workers. "It's a big unit; that's a large number of workers," said Eduardo R. Blanco of the ALRB. "Clearly [the negotiations] went very smoothly and very quickly." Rodriguez said that the agreement, which included one-third of the rose workers in California, was "historic," and added that the company "was willing to meet its workers' needs."[73]

Meanwhile, Rodriguez and Huerta were negotiating a new contract with Bruce Church, Inc. Much of the bitterness between the company and the UFW had disappeared with the death of César Chávez. The new contract was signed at the César Chávez Library in Salinas, California. The UFW won pay increases for the workers that would reach more than $8.50 per hour in 2001. The UFW and the Bruce Church company also agreed to work together to control the use of pesticides in the fields. In addition, Church provided health insurance for its workers.

At the same time, the UFW continued its efforts to sign up more strawberry workers in California. "At this point, it's like a motherhood campaign," Huerta said. "We're asking for job security, health care, a medical plan, and end to sexual

BEING HISPANIC

A TIRELESS WORKER FOR ALL PEOPLE

Dolores Huerta has been called a leader of the Chicano/Chicana movement in the United States. Beginning in the 1960s, there was an effort to recognize the important contributions of Mexican Americans. But Huerta resists being identified only with the issues that affect Mexican Americans. Instead, she sees herself as an activist—someone who shows all "people how to work together and take on the issues affecting them."

Both her parents were role models for the type of life that Huerta chose for herself. Her father was a labor organizer who tried to improve the working conditions of the miners in New Mexico. Her mother, Alicia, was a successful businessperson who also raised a family. Huerta realized that she could do both, unlike most Hispanic women who were expected to be wives and mothers. She also learned from her mother that no person, no matter how poor, should be turned away. Everyone was entitled to be treated equally and with respect for his/her dignity.

Huerta was guided by these values during her career as a union organizer. While the National Farm Workers were primarily Mexican Americans, Huerta believed that her mission was to improve the lives of all working people, regardless of their ethnic backgrounds. Eleanor Smeal, president of the Feminist Majority Foundation, once explained that Huerta "is the hardest working, most determined yet optimistic crusader for people I have met. She is tireless." This work transcends the needs of Mexican Americans and applies to all people who are looking for dignity. "My message," Huerta says, "is one of social justice. That means we have to take into account workers, students of color . . . African Americans and Latinos."

harassment." Although the union continued to win elections, growers still dragged their feet when it came to negotiating and signing contracts. A spokesman for the growers pointed out: "The farms where they won elections were financially in trouble. Union or no union, those farms could have easily gone out of business anyway." Huerta countered, "They've all gotten workers cheaply. They've all become wealthy." The UFW also led a boycott of strawberries in supermarkets, using the slogan "5 cents for fairness." This was an appeal to shoppers to pay an additional five cents for a package of strawberries so the workers who picked them could be paid a better wage.[74]

While dealing with the strawberry workers, the UFW also led an organizing effort against the large Gallo Vineyard. In 1994, workers selected the UFW to represent them at Gallo. The company tried to delay contract negotiations as long as possible. In 2000, the UFW and Gallo finally signed a contract that included higher wages and vacation benefits. The UFW was clearly moving forward again.

8

Battling for Justice

During the early part of the twenty-first century, Dolores Huerta continued fighting for the rights of farmworkers. Meanwhile, the UFW also continued to increase its membership and expand its power base in the union movement.

AGE DOES NOT STOP HUERTA

In 2000, Dolores Huerta turned 70 years old. Despite her advancing age, she did not slow her pace or reduce the number of her speaking engagements. Huerta spoke in front of large audiences, usually wearing a red beret and dressed in black and red—the colors of the UFW. Her talks described the efforts of the late César Chávez to lead the struggle of the farmworkers for better working conditions. After finishing her speech, Huerta would usually walk among the crowd, talking to as many people as possible. As Huerta told an interviewer, "There is just so much work to be done, and someone has to do it.

Even after the turn of the twenty-first century, Dolores Huerta and the farmworkers she supports continue to march for better working conditions. Huerta is pictured here with UFW President Arturo Rodriguez (right) during a march to Sacramento in August 2002.

In organizing, you are not going to reach every person, but you just have to keep pushing for the next one."[75]

Huerta's speaking engagements included events in Florida, where she spoke to a group of farmworkers represented by the UFW. She also went to the California state capitol at Sacramento to lobby for new legislation to reduce the use of pesticides in the fields. Huerta retired as secretary-treasurer of the UFW in 2000, hoping to reduce her day-to-day responsibilities for the union. Nevertheless, her travels on behalf of the farmworkers did not decline.

GROWTH OF THE UFW

The UFW continued to increase its membership. In 2000, the union won an election to represent additional strawberry workers in California. Two years later, as a result of UFW lob-bying efforts in Sacramento, the California legislature passed a new law that was an enormous victory for the union. The law required mediation from the Agricultural Labor Relations Board if growers wouldn't agree to a contract with the UFW. "I'm very pleased," said Assemblyman Tony Cardenas, a sup-porter of the bill. "I think the Latino community is going to show a lot of appreciation for this."[76]

In 2004, the new mediation law had an important impact on UFW organizing efforts. The union was negotiating with a mushroom farm owned by Pictsweet in Ventura, California. The negotiations had occurred after several years of picketing and boycotts. However, Pictsweet was still reluctant to negoti-ate with the UFW. Under the new law, the UFW called in a labor mediator who came up with a new agreement for 300 workers. "This is historic," said UFW President Arturo Rodriguez. "I give tremendous credit to the workers at Pictsweet—they had the resolve and commitment to really bring about change for themselves and their families."[77]

However, the work of the UFW was not limited to helping farmworkers win new contracts. Under Rodriguez's leadership, the union has greatly expanded its activities in support of Mexican Americans and other Hispanic immigrant groups. Collectively, these people are known as the Latino community. They make up the fastest-growing segment of the U.S. popula-tion. Although many Latinos live in rural areas, more and more of these immigrants live in cities. Many Latinos live in Los Angeles, San Antonio, and other cities, especially in the southwestern and western United States.

Even though many Latinos have moved away from rural areas, they often remember the UFW and its leaders, César Chávez and Dolores Huerta. Under Arturo Rodriguez, the UFW has gone into the cities to help Latinos. In places like Albuquerque, New Mexico, and Fresno, California, the UFW built inexpensive housing for many people who used to be farm laborers. More than 200 housing units have been developed in

Albuquerque, and more than 500 in Fresno. In addition, the UFW has been working to provide affordable housing in Phoenix and in Dallas. According to César's son Paul Chávez, the "Latino community is the most urbanized minority in this country. . . . Who is our customer? Yes, it's farmworkers, and we will always serve them. But if we look at future growth, the Latino urban community is where it's at."[78]

Many Latinos are struggling for equal rights, and the UFW has been helping them. In 2000, members of the newsroom at Channel 21—a Spanish-speaking television station in Fresno, California—were protesting that they received lower salaries than comparable employees at English-speaking stations. At first, the newsroom employees asked for help from their own union, the National Association of Broadcast Employees and Technicians. The union, however, was unable to convince the owner of the station—Univision—to increase salaries.

Some of the employees at Channel 21 were the children of farmworkers who had been organized by the UFW. The UFW also had a close relationship with the Univision chief executive officer, Henry Cisneros. A former secretary of housing during the 1990s, Cisneros had supported the efforts of the UFW. He had worked closely with Huerta and Chávez. The employees at Channel 21 finally turned to the UFW for help.

One of the Channel 21 employees was Reina Cardenas, who had gone on a hunger strike to protest her working conditions. Her parents were farmworkers. As Cardenas's mother put it, "The UFW is giving importance to their [contract dispute] by supporting them. . . . The UFW has always encouraged farmworker children to advance, to move forward."

The UFW organized rallies outside the television station and called on viewers to boycott Channel 21. UFW pickets also went to Cisneros's home. According to *Los Angeles Times* reporter Dana Calvo, the "public opposition embarrassed Cisneros and tested an old friendship." As a result, Univision agreed to a new contract that increased the salaries of the newsroom employees at Channel 21, although the salaries still fell short of those of workers at English-speaking stations. Paul Chávez hailed the UFW victory, saying it brought together traditional farmworkers and their children, who have moved on to other types of jobs. "Working in the fields leaves an impact on people that lasts for generations,"[79] he said.

THE TRIALS OF DOLORES HUERTA

While the UFW was growing and expanding its influence, Dolores Huerta was confined to a hospital bed. Late in 2000, she had been admitted to a hospital with an aneurysm, a weakening in a blood vessel. Huerta's aneurysm occurred near her heart, which could have killed her, and it reoccurred in her intestines. She was forced to spend the next year recovering. By 2002, however, she had begun to return to her normal routine of speaking to community groups and other activists.

In December 2002, Huerta was awarded the Puffin Prize by the Nation Institute. This prize, totaling $100,000, is given to someone who has spent his or her career working on behalf of social justice. Huerta said that she hoped to spend the money to train more activists. "We need an organizers' institute,"[80] she explained.

In 2003, Huerta was appointed by California Governor Gray Davis as a member of the University of California's Board of Regents. This committee oversees the operations of the California public university system. Fred Ross, Jr.—son of Huerta's mentor—said, "She will be an outstanding representative for the disenfranchised, the sons and daughters of farmworkers and the urban poor, and a tireless advocate for diversity in the university."[81] Huerta herself added, "My message is one of social justice. That means we have to take into account workers, students of color. We can look at the numbers of African Americans and Latinos and we don't see their numbers at the university in proportion to their population in the state. We should change that."[82]

Huerta's work has not only been on behalf of people of color. She has also tried to broaden opportunities for women.

Dolores Huerta has worked closely with California Governor Gray Davis, who appointed her to serve as a member of the state's Board of Regents in 2003. Huerta and Davis are pictured together here at a labor rally in San Francisco in September 2003.

Throughout her career, she was forced to fight female stereotypes. Former governor Jerry Brown once described Huerta as "embodying the spirit of César Chávez." Indeed, she often walked in Chávez's shadow. Although many biographies have been written about Chávez, no full-length biography has been written about Dolores Huerta. As Huerta put it, "At some point in my career in the union I realized that women were not being valued for what they were doing. . . . Women have the ideas and men take the credit for them. It happens all the time."[83]

Huerta started an organization, the Dolores Huerta Foundation, in 2003, after winning the Puffin Award, to train community activists. Part of its work is to encourage women to

A CIRCLE OF FRIENDS

DOLORES HUERTA AND THE DEMOCRATIC PARTY

Throughout her career, Dolores Huerta has worked closely with some of the most powerful political leaders in the United States. Among them was Robert F. Kennedy, who ran his brother John F. Kennedy's successful campaign for president of the United States in 1960. In 1968, Kennedy made his own run for president with strong support from the UFW. Huerta and the UFW helped Kennedy win the Democratic primary election in California, held on June 4, 1968. Late that evening, Kennedy was assassinated.

A few years later, Dolores Huerta provided strong support to another Democratic politician, Governor Jerry Brown of California. Huerta worked closely with Brown in Sacramento in 1975 to secure the passage of the Agricultural Labor Relations Act. This law greatly improved the bargaining position of the UFW in contract negotiations. Brown also received UFW support when he sought the Democratic nomination for president. Governor Brown made several unsuccessful campaigns for president of the United States, in 1976, 1980, and 1992.

In 1992, Bill Clinton won the Democratic nomination for president and later that year became our country's 42nd Chief of State. In 1999, Clinton gave Dolores Huerta the Eleanor Roosevelt Human Rights Award for her work as a lifelong labor activist.

Although Dolores Huerta has known many powerful political leaders, her friends have also included famous entertainers. Among them are the folk singer Joan Baez, whose father was a Mexican scientist, and Mexican-American guitarist Carlos Santana. Along with his band, Santana, the guitarist has recorded many jazz and rock-and-roll hits. In 1999, he played at a celebration for Dolores Huerta, honoring her work with the UFW.

Dolores Huerta continues to work hard for the causes she believes in. In 2004, she played an active role in the presidential campaign of Democrat John Kerry.

become involved in community organizing. "Young women have to learn to build up the emotional strength they need to fight for themselves, for other women, and for their communities," she said in an interview in 2005. "They need to run for office and get elected. If we don't have women at the decision-making table, then we know that the table is going to make wrong decisions. We have a different energy, a different intellect, and, as women, we like to get the job done."[84]

Although Huerta has campaigned for the rights of women in recent years, she has never forgotten her commitment to America's farmworkers. As she said in a speech in 2005, "Farmworkers do the most sacred work of all. They put food out on the table. They should be treated better than anyone else, not worse."[85] Huerta began her career as an activist in the farmworker movement in the 1950s, and her commitment to that struggle has never ended.

Chronology and Timeline

1930	Dolores Huerta born on April 10 in Dawson, New Mexico.
1936	Huerta's parents divorce; moves with her mother to Stockton, California.
1941–1945	The United States fights in World War II; Huerta sells war bonds in Stockton.
1947	Graduates from Stockton High School.
1950	Marries Ralph Head.
1953–1955	Works as a schoolteacher.
1955	Joins Community Service Organization (CSO), a grassroots organization founded by Fred Ross.
1958	Joins Agricultural Workers Association.
1960	While working for the Community Service Organization, Huerta founds the Agricultural Workers Association (ASO).
1961	Thanks to her lobbying efforts, Huerta succeeds in helping to do away with citizenship requirements for pension and public assistance programs for legal residents of the United States.
1962	Farm Workers Association (FWA) holds its first convention.
1965	Grape strike begins in Delano, California; more than 5,000 workers walk off the job in a strike that will last five years.
1966	Huerta joins the Farm Workers Association.
1966–1970	Negotiates contracts between FWA and grape growers.
1967	The Agricultural Workers Organizing Committee (AWOC) and the National Farm Workers Association (NFWA) merge to become the United Farm Workers Organizing Committee (UFWOC).
1968	On the same day he wins the Democratic presidential nomination, Robert F. Kennedy is assassinated.

1970–1975	United Farm Workers battles Teamsters Union.
1973	United Farm Workers (UFW) is formed, led by Chávez and Huerta.
1974	Instrumental in securing unemployment benefits for farmworkers.
1975	California passes Agricultural Labor Relations Act, which grants farmworkers the right to collectively organize and bargain for better wages.
1979	Helps lead massive lettuce strike.
1984	New boycott begins, aimed at removing pesticides from fields; Huerta wins Outstanding Labor Leader Award.
1986	Helps win passage of new immigration law.
1988	Injured during demonstration against George H. W. Bush in San Francisco.

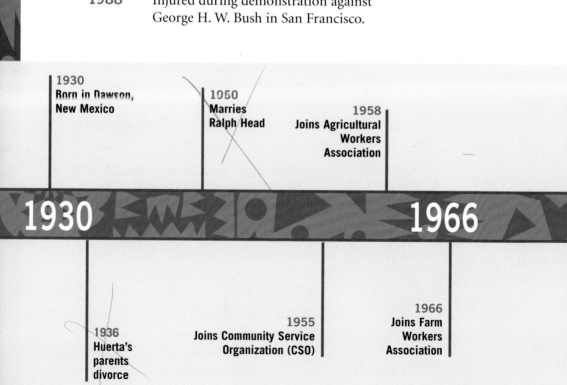

1930
Born in Dawson, New Mexico

1950
Marries Ralph Head

1958
Joins Agricultural Workers Association

1930

1966

1936
Huerta's parents divorce

1955
Joins Community Service Organization (CSO)

1966
Joins Farm Workers Association

1993	César Chávez dies; Arturo Rodriguez heads UFW; Huerta inducted into National Women's Hall of Fame in Seneca Falls, New York; also receives the American Civil Liberties Union (ACLU) Roger Baldwin Medal of Liberty Award, the Eugene V. Debs Foundation Outstanding American Award, and the Ellis Island Medal of Freedom Award.
1995	Huerta negotiates new union contracts with growers.
1998	Receives the United States Presidential Eleanor D. Roosevelt Human Rights Award from President Bill Clinton.
2000	Hospitalized with aneurysm.
2002	Awarded Puffin Prize for career in social activism.
2003	Begins institute to train social activists; appointed to California Board of Regents; receives a short-term appointment as a University of California Regent.

1966–1970
Negotiates contracts between NFWA and grape growers

1979
Helps lead massive lettuce strike

1993
Inducted into National Women's Hall of Fame

1970

2002

1973
Formation of United Farm Workers (UFW)

1986
Helps win passage of new immigration law

2002
Awarded Puffin Prize for career in social activism

Notes

Chapter 1

1 Susan Ferriss and Ricardo Sandoval, *The Fight in the Fields: Cesar Chavez and the Farmworkers Movement* (New York: Harcourt Brace, 1997), 105.

2 Marshall Ganz, "The Power of Story in Social Movements," Cambridge, Mass.: Kennedy School of Government, 2001.

3 Jacques Levy, *Cesar Chavez: Autobiography of La Causa* (New York: W. W. Norton, 1975), 224.

4 Ferriss and Sandoval, 136.

5 Levy, 262.

6 J. Craig Jenkins, *The Politics of Insurgency: The Farm Worker Movement in the 1960s* (New York: Columbia University Press, 1985), 163.

7 Levy, 277.

8 Jenkins, 170.

9 Wayne Moquin and Charles Van Doren, eds., *A Documentary History of the Mexican Americans* (New York: Praeger, 1971), 364.

10 Jenkins, 172.

Chapter 2

11 Lisa Genasci, "UFW Co-Founder Comes Out of Shadow," *Los Angeles Times*, May 11, 1995. Available online at *http://proquest.umi.com/pqdweb?index=46&did=21431044&SrchMode=i&sid=1&Fmt=3*

12 Frank Perez, *Dolores Huerta* (Austin, Tex.: Raintree Steck-Vaughn, 1996), 13.

13 Katherine King, "Just Do It," *New Moon*, Jan/Feb 2005, 18.

14 Perez, 14.

15 James Rainey, "The Eternal Soldadera," *Los Angeles Times Magazine*, August 15, 1999.

16 Richard Griswold Del Castillo and Richard Garcia, *Cesar Chavez, A Triumph of the Spirit* (Norman, Okla.: University of Oklahoma Press, 1995), 64.

17 "Dolores Huerta." Available online at *http://www.theglassceiling.com/biographies/bio15.htm.*

18 Ibid.

19 Ibid.

Chapter 3

20 David Bacon, "El Valiente Chicano." Available online at *http://www.cc-ds.org/Labor/Chicano.htm.*

21 J. Craig Jenkins, *The Politics of Insurgency: The Farm Worker Movement in the 1960s* (New York: Columbia University Press, 1985), 78.

22 Ferriss and Sandoval, 16–17.

23 Ibid., 10.

24 Del Castillo and Garcia, 15.

25 Ferriss and Sandoval, 28.

26 "Small Man with a Big Dream," from Jan Young's *Cesar Chavez & the Migrant Farmworkers* (New York: Messner, 1972). Available online at *http://www.sfsu.edu/~cecipp/cesar_chavez/smallmanbigdream.htm.*

27 Ibid., 29.

28 Ferriss and Sandoval, 61.

29 Lu Herrera, "For the Sake of Good," *Hispanic*, May 2003.

30 Perez, 20–21.

31 Del Castillo and Garcia, 31.

32 Ferriss and Sandoval, 70.

33 Ibid., 62.

Chapter 4

34 Jenkins, 135.

35 Ibid.

36 Ganz, "The Power of Story in Social Movements."

37 Ferriss and Sandoval, 77.
38 Jacques Levy, *Cesar Chavez* (New York: W. W. Norton, 1975), 163.
39 Ferriss and Sandoval, 77.
40 Jenkins, 140–141.
41 Ferriss and Sandoval, 81.
42 Jenkins, 145.
43 Ferriss and Sandoval, 89.

Chapter 5
44 Del Castillo and Garcia, 62.
45 Ibid., 63.
46 Ibid., 70.
47 Jenkins, 187.
48 Ferriss and Sandoval, 169.
49 Levy, 392.
50 Jenkins, 189.
51 Del Castillo and Gracia, 124.

Chapter 6
52 Jenkins, 205.
53 Levy, 264–265.
54 James Rainey, "The Eternal Soldadera," *Los Angeles Times*, August 15, 1999.
55 Ibid.
56 Ibid.
57 Lisa Genasci, "UFW Co-Founder Comes Out of Shadow," *Los Angeles Times*, May 11, 1995.
58 Ibid.
59 Rainey, "The Eternal Soldadera."
60 Harvey Bernstein, "Workers Can't Expect a Fair Shake from the Farm Board," *Los Angeles Times*, December 8, 1987.
61 Ferriss and Sandoval, 244.
62 Louis Sahagun, "Three of Robert Kennedy's Children Visit Chavez to Support Protest," *Los Angeles Times*, August 5, 1988.
63 Harry Bernstein, "Tough Row to Hoe for Most Farm Workers Still Mired in Poverty," *Los Angeles Times*, July 25, 1985.

Chapter 7
64 Miles Corwin, "The Grapes of Wrath Revisited," *Los Angeles Times*, September 29, 1991.
65 Mark Arax and Jenifer Warren, "Chavez's Season of Gain for Farm Workers Slips Away," *Los Angeles Times*, April 29, 1993.
66 Patrick J. McDonnell, "Chavez's Mission Will Continue, Say Farm Workers Union Leaders," *Los Angeles Times*, April 25, 1993.
67 Ferriss and Sandoval, 257.
68 McDonnell, "Chavez's Mission Will Continue."
69 Arthur Jones, "Building Strength," *National Catholic Reporter*, April 18, 2003.
70 Mark Arax, "Union's Focus on Fields Starts to Bear Fruit," *Los Angeles Times*, July 18, 1994.
71 Scott Hadly, "UFW Steps Up Organizing Efforts in Area," *Los Angeles Times*, September 7, 1994.
72 Ferriss and Sandoval, 274.
73 Michael Parrish, "With New Pact, Union Takes Big Step Back to Prominence," *Los Angeles Times*, March 18, 1995.
74 Pat Broderick, "Fearless Organizer Fights for Strawberry Workers," *San Diego Business Journal*, April 7, 1997.

Chapter 8
75 James Rainey, "The Eternal Soldadera," *Los Angeles Times*, August 15, 1999.
76 Gregg Jones, "A Big Win for Farm Workers," *Los Angeles Times*, October 1, 2002.
77 Fred Alvarez, "Pictsweet Workers Win Contract," *Los Angeles Times*, February 18, 2004.

78 Dana Calvo, "UFW Toils in a New Field: Cities," *Los Angeles Times*, May 26, 2000.

79 Ibid.

80 Tom Hayden, "Prize for Dolores Huerta," *Nation*, December 23, 2002.

81 Rebecca Trounson, et al, "Add Fiery Regent and Stir the Board," *Los Angeles Times*, September 12, 2003.

82 Ibid.

83 Lisa Genasci, "UFW Co-Founder Comes Out of Shadow," *Los Angeles Times*, May 11, 1995.

84 Katherine King, "Just Do It," *New Moon*, January/February, 2005.

85 Jennifer C. Smith, "United Farm Workers Co-Founder Gives Rousing Speech for Members' Benefits," *The Monitor*, February 26, 2005.

Bibliography

Del Castillo, Richard Griswold, and Richard Garcia. *César Chávez: A Triumph of Spirit*. Norman, Okla.: University of Oklahoma Press, 1995.

Ferriss, Susan, and Ricardo Sandoval. *The Fight in the Fields: César Chávez and the Farmworkers Movement*. New York: Harcourt Brace, 1997.

Gonzales, Manuel. *Mexicanos: A History of Mexicans in the United States*. Bloomington, Ind.: University of Indiana Press, 1999.

Jenkins, J. Craig. *The Politics of Insurgency: The Farm Worker Movement in the 1960s*. New York: Columbia University Press, 1985.

Levy, Jacques. *César Chávez: Autobiography of La Causa*. New York: W. W. Norton, 1975.

Moquin, Wayne, and Charles Van Doren, eds. *A Documentary History of the Mexican Americans*. New York: Praeger, 1971.

Further Reading

Altman, Linda Jacobs. *The Importance of César Chávez*. San Diego, Calif.: Lucent Books, 1996.

Bowdish, Lynea. *With Courage: Seven Women Who Changed America*. San Jose, Calif.: Mondo, 2004.

Dunne, John Gregory. *Delano: The Story of the California Grape Strike*. New York: Farrar, Straus and Giroux, 1976.

Hacker, Carlotta. *Humanitarians*. New York: Crabtree, 1999.

Perez, Frank. *Dolores Huerta*. Austin, Tex.: Raintree Steck-Vaughn, 1996.

Web sites

The Cesar Chavez Foundation
http://cesarechavezfoundation.org/

The Dolores Huerta Foundation
http://www.doloreshuerta.org/dolores_huerta_foundation.htm

Article on the Dolores Huerta Foundation
*http://www.pinnaclenews.com/sv-edition/
story.php?section=stories_sv_archived&id=153*

United Farm Workers of America
http://www.ufw.org/

Article on Dolores Huerta Being Named Ms. Magazine's Woman of the Year
http://www.ufw.org/ms.htm

Index

Adair, Doug, 45–46
AFL-CIO, 36–37
Agricultural Labor
    Relations Act (ALRA),
    58–61, 86
Agricultural Labor
    Relations Board
    (ALRB), 59, 69, 82
Agricultural Workers
    Association, 33, 36, 37
Agricultural Workers
    Organizing Committee
    (AWOC), 36–37, 47
American Federation of
    Labor (ALF), 24, 29,
    36–37

Baez, Joan, 86
bananas, 52–53
Bank, John, 56
barrios, 28
Bear Creek Production
    Company, 77
birthday, 17
Bloody Christmas, 34
Board of Regents, 84
Border Patrol, 41
boycotts, 12–16, 51–54,
    68–69, 74, 79
Bracero Program, 22–23,
    30, 34–35, 38, 41
Brown, Edmund G., 11
Brown, Jerry, 56–58, 86
Bruce Church, Inc., 74–75,
    77
Bush, George H. W., 72

campesinos, 20
Cardenas, Reina, 83
Catholic Bishops'
    Committee, 52
Chávez, Camilla (daugh-
    ter), 67
Chávez, César
    death of, 74–76
    disagreements with,
    66–67

fast of, 13–14
FWA and, 39–47
life of, 30–35
management by, 65–66
march of, 11
NFWA and, 7
Teamsters Union and,
    51–53
Chávez, Helen, 32, 48–49
Chávez, Juanita (daugh-
    ter), 67
Chávez, Librado, 30–31
Chávez, Maria Elena
    (daughter), 67
Chávez, Richard, 31–32,
    67, 75
Chávez, Ricky (son), 67
Chicano/Chicana move-
    ment, 64, 78
Chiquita bananas, 52–53
Cisneros, Henry, 83
citizenship, 70
Clinton, William J., 86
Communism, 9, 33
Community Service
    Organization (CSO),
    32–35, 35–38
Congress of Industrial
    Organizations (CIO),
    24, 36–37
Congress of Racial
    Equality, 9
contratistas, 20
Contreras, Rufino, 63
co-ops, 41–42
Corona, Bert, 29–30
coyotes, 31, 37
credit unions, 36, 41, 43

Davis, Gray, 84, 85
De la Cruz, Juan and
    Maximina, 55
Delano, California, 6–11,
    46–47
Deukmejian, George,
    68–69
Díaz, Porfirio, 19

DiGiorgio Fruit
    Corporation, 11–13
Dole Food Company, 77
Dolores Huerta
    Foundation, 85–86
Drake, Jim, 43

Eleanor Roosevelt Human
    Rights Award, 86

Fabela, Helen. *See* Chávez,
    Helen
Farm Labor Organizing
    Committee, 76
Farm Workers Association
    (FWA), 39–42, 42–45,
    45–47
fasting, 13–14, 71, 83
Federal Office of
    Economic
    Opportunity, 45
Fernandez, Alicia (moth-
    er), 17, 20–22, 24–25,
    49–50, 78
Fernandez, John (brother),
    20, 21
Fernandez, Juan (father),
    17, 19–20, 25
Fernandez, Marshall
    (brother), 20, 21
Filipinos, 6–11, 46–47
fines, 70
Florida, 58
Fresh Pict, 53

Gallo Vineyards, 55,
    57–58, 79
Ganz, Marshall, 66, 68
Garza, Ben, 28–29
goon squads, 52, 53
grapes, 6–11, 46–47,
    54–56, 68–69
Great Migration, 19–20
green carders, 40, 46
Guimarra Vineyards,
    13–14, 55

Hartmire, Chris, 43
Hazen, David, 43
Head, Celeste (daughter), 25
Head, Lori (daughter), 25
Head, Ralph (husband), 25
Healy, Dorothy Ray, 25
housing, 82–83
Huerta, Alicia (daughter), 37
Huerta, Angela (daughter), 37
Huerta, Emilio (son), 37
Huerta, Fidel (son), 37, 71
Huerta, Ventura (husband), 37–38
Huerta, Vincent (son), 37

illegal aliens, 40–41, 70, 73–74
insurance, 41, 62
InterHarvest, 52–53
International Longshore and Warehouse Union, 29

Johnson, Lyndon B., 45

Kennedy, Ethel, 53
Kennedy, John F., 45
Kennedy, Robert F., 14, 15, 86
Kerry, John, 87
Ku Klux Klan, 63–65
KUFW, 67

Lauer, Will, 52–53
League of United Latin American Citizens (LULAC), 28–29
legislation, 56–61, 81–82
lettuce, 50–54, 62–65, 74
Longshore Union, 29
Lucky Supermarkets, 74

marches, 11, 76
Marciel, Juan, 74
McCarthyism, 33–35
McCullough, Thomas, 36, 37
McDonnell, Donald, 32
mediation, 82
Mendoza, Juan, 73–74
Mexico, 19–20, 69–70
Migrant Ministry, 43
migration, 19–20, 69–70
mining, 19–20
Moreno, Luisa, 24, 25
mushrooms, 82
mutualistas, 28, 42

National Association of Broadcast Employees and Technicians, 83
National Council of Churches, 43
National Farm Workers Association (NFWA), 7, 8
New Mexico, 17–20, 25
newspapers, 45–46
Nixon, Richard, 15

Our Lady of Guadalupe Church, 47

pesticides, 68, 77
Pic N Pac, 53
Pictsweet, 82
Proposition 14, 60–61
Puffin Prize, 84, 85
Purex Company, 53

Radio Campesina, 67
Reagan, Ronald, 56, 68
Retail Clerks and Butchers Union, 54
Richards, James (stepfather), 21–22
Rios, Antonio, 34
Rodriguez, Arturo, 76–77, 82

Rodriguez, Marta, 55–56
Roosevelt, Franklin D., 23
roses, 46
Ross, Fred, 32–33, 34, 52
Ross Jr., Fred, 84

Santana, Carlos, 86
scabs, 8–9, 11–12, 13–14, 63
Schenley Company, 7–11
schools, 25, 28–29
segregation, 28–29
Senate Subcommittee on Migratory Labor, 10–11
Sotaco, Don, 45–46
Stockton, California, 20–21, 25
strawberries, 77, 79, 81–82
strikes
  AWOC and, 37
  in Delano, California, 6–11, 46–47
  DiGiorgio Fruit Corporation and, 11–13
  grape boycott and, 12–16
  lettuce and, 62–65
  rose workers and, 46
  Teamsters Union and, 51

teaching, 25–26, 43, 64
Teamsters Union, 12, 50–53, 53–56, 59–61
Teatro Campesino, 10

UCA-PAWA, 24, 25
unions, 10, 12, 29, 38. See also Teamsters Union
United Auto Workers Union, 10
United Farm Workers of America (UFW)
  decline of, 71
  farmworkers and, 73–74
  growth of, 74–79, 81–84
  legislation and, 56–59

new leadership of,
76–79
problems of, 65–68
success of, 62–65
union difficulties and,
68–70
United Farm Workers
Organizing Committee

(UFWOC), 47, 48–50,
50–53, 53–56
United Fruit Company,
52–53
Univision, 83–84

Valdez, Luis, 10, 50
Valenzuela, Frank, 55

Velasquez, Baldemar, 76
violence, 55–56, 63, 72
vote, 32–33, 36
War on Poverty, 45
Wilson, Pete, 74
Women's Hall of Fame,
64
World War II, 22–23

Picture Credits

About the Author

Richard Worth is a writer and corporate trainer with more than 25 years experience writing young adult nonfiction. He has written for a variety of publishers and has published more than 50 books in biography, history, current events, and the criminal justice system. His book *Gangs and Crime* was included on the New York Public Library's 2003 Best Books for the Teen Age List. Some of his Chelsea House titles include *Pervez Musharraf* (MAJOR WORLD LEADERS), *Independence for Latino America* (LATINO-AMERICAN HISTORY), and *Dalai Lama* (SPIRITUAL LEADERS AND THINKERS).